I0521581

The Proven Path to Self-Compassion

Discover the Power of Self-Love, Self-Care and Mindfulness

Zera Young

Contents

Get Your Ebook Stop Limiting Yourself
+ Reduce Stress in 1 minute [video]
+ Printable Gratitude Journal

 +  +

Scan the QR code below to claim your free bonuses

——————————— **OR** ———————————

visit gifts.zerayoung.com/compassion

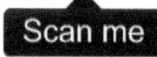

Unleash your true potential and choose to live your best life!

✔Free e-book: Stop Limiting Yourself. Stop doubting your potential and learn to recognize your self-limiting beliefs!

✔Free meditation video: Reduce your stress levels in one minute with this powerful breathing exercise.

✔Printable Journal: Print out your daily and monthly Personal Gratitude Journal for positive manifestation and improved self-confidence!

Get My Audiobook for FREE

If you love listening to audiobooks on the go, you can download the audiobook version of my book *Set Good Boundaries* for FREE (Regularly $14.95) just by signing up for a FREE 30-day Audible trial!

Follow the QR codes below to get started

Audible US

Audible UK

Introduction

*"Self-compassion is simply giving the same kindness
to ourselves that we would give to others."*

— Christopher Germer

Throughout our lives, we learn to show sympathy and
support our loved ones when they're feeling unworthy or
facing challenging times. We know how to ask "What do
you need?", offer help, and reassure them that they always
can count on us. We speak gently and with kindness, using
nonverbal cues like a warm embrace or a steady hand on
their shoulder to show we care. And when necessary, we
take swift and decisive action to protect our loved ones. We
feel a surge of energy when they are in danger and need our
protection, and we help them overcome obstacles with a
little nudge. Through experience, we have mastered the
insight and skills to be there for others in all kinds of
situations.

Unfortunately, we don't often show ourselves the same compassion and understanding when faced with adversity. Instead of pausing to ask ourselves what we need in the moment and providing comfort and support, we may be more prone to judgment, problem-solving, or panic. When we spill coffee on our way to work, we instantly berate ourselves for being too clumsy or stupid. But would we ever do that to a close friend? It's interesting to note how frequently we speak to ourselves in this negative way and yet still find ways to justify it.

Self-criticism and unattainable standards prevent us from giving ourselves the respect we deserve, stifling our emotions and leaving us feeling unsafe and lonely. When we are hard on ourselves, we go into defense mode. We can't make a mistake, or else we'll shower ourselves with insults. What some of us are not realizing is that this constant stream of low-level stress is harming our minds, hearts, and bodies.

Believing that survival depends on maintaining perfect control over every aspect of our lives might trap us in an endless circle of suffering. It has the potential to paralyze us, preventing us from going after our goals. Overwhelmed by negative thoughts and feelings, we may act in ways inconsistent with our ideals, leading to more self-criticism and perpetuating the cycle of negativity. By failing to acknowledge the damage we cause by our negative self-talk and succumbing to it, we risk getting stuck in a never-ending loop and ultimately losing all our self-esteem.

This type of negativity prevents us from reaching our full potential and greatly impacts our mental and emotional well-being. But we don't have to keep being our worst enemy; we can learn to be as kind to ourselves as we are to others. Imagine how much better we would feel if we could let go of those negative thoughts and treat ourselves with the same compassion.

This book offers insight into the importance of self-compassion and provides research-backed methods for developing it. By reading this book and implementing its guidance, you can work toward a more compassionate relationship with yourself. You'll learn how to manage self-criticism and cultivate self-compassion, which will decrease your levels of stress and anxiety significantly.

Self-compassion is the practice of being kind and understanding toward yourself despite your flaws and even when you make mistakes. It means recognizing that you deserve love and compassion no matter what, just like anyone else. It's a supportive inner voice that encourages you to be kind to yourself and take care of yourself. Self-compassion helps you find hope in difficult times and fully enjoy your successes in times of bliss.

Contrary to popular belief, self-compassion is not a complex mental exercise that can only be attained by monks who practiced years of meditation. It's something that we can all cultivate and train. By being kind and understanding friends to ourselves, we can develop self-compassion and experience its many benefits.

Being compassionate and caring are human tendencies that come naturally and give us a lot in return. It's not about being perfect but rather about finding ways to support ourselves and cope with life's challenges. By prioritizing self-care and happiness over perfectionism and anxiety, we develop a healthier, more compassionate, and more understanding relationship with ourselves. And while self-compassion won't solve all of our problems, it can help us to better navigate difficult times and emotions.

By showing yourself kindness and understanding, you can approach your mistakes with curiosity and with a desire to learn and improve rather than judge and blame. This can be extremely useful when you have done something you feel bad about or something that is out of alignment with your values. Instead of judging yourself harshly, you can say to yourself, "I made a mistake, but that doesn't make me a bad person, and it's just a reminder that I need to make some changes."

Take note that self-compassion is not about absolving yourself from responsibility; it's about recognizing that you are worthy of care and support even when you make mistakes and that you can make positive changes in your life at any given moment.

There may be countless new opportunities uncovered by using this strategy. Imagine how you'd feel if you went about your day knowing you deserve kindness and compassion at all times, enabling you to tackle each difficulty more positively. Think of all the possibilities that would arise in your personal and professional life if you would fully embrace this way of thinking. Our critical voice discourages us from putting ourselves out there, taking chances, and making meaningful connections with others, but self-compassion can give us the courage and confidence we so desperately need in these situations.

This book will teach you how to cultivate compassion through mindfulness techniques and other 'staying present'-strategies. By learning to let go of distractions and identifying the sources of negativity in your life, you can become kinder to yourself when it matters most. These techniques can help you become more self-aware and make you better able to respond to your own needs with compassion and care.

To get the most out of this book, approach it with the following mindset: instead of thinking of yourself as broken and in need of fixing, try viewing yourself as perfectly imperfect, just as you are. Adopting this mindset will make your experience a lot easier and more enjoyable. This book will assist you in dealing with emotional pain from a place of kindness and love.

To get good at something, you need to practice it a lot. Doing the exercises regularly and putting in the time and effort to practice self-compassion is essential. The more you practice and the more consistent you are, the better you will get at it. It's recommended to practice for at least 30 minutes daily, but if that's not possible, don't stress about it, do what feels reasonable and manageable for you.

Remember that everyone is different and what works for one person may not work for another. If something you read in this book doesn't feel helpful or valuable to you, feel free to adjust, personalize, or even skip it; a different chapter or approach may resonate with you more. I do encourage you to try everything at least once and with full dedication. What may feel cumbersome or challenging initially may eventually become liberating and helpful. Be open to trying new things and applying what you learn; you may discover valuable new ways of doing things you never deemed possible. It's also important to recognize that some exercises may bring up difficult emotions or thoughts, as they ask us to confront our challenges directly. This is a normal part of the process, but it's crucial to take care of yourself and move at a comfortable pace.

By working with this guide, you have already taken an important step toward a happier, healthier, and more self-compassionate life. Self-compassion can profoundly impact your well-being, as I have seen firsthand in my work with clients and personal experience. Through my years of practice, I have witnessed its transformative power in helping people learn to love themselves, no matter their achievements or how challenging things may be.

I am excited to support you on your journey and hope you will experience the same sense of freedom and fulfillment that my clients have found through this practice. As we embark on this journey together, I wish you the best as you actively cultivate love, warmth, kindness, compassion, and joy for yourself and others. Let's get started!

1. What is Self-Compassion?

Self-compassion–being supportive and kind to yourself, especially in the face of stress and failure–is associated with more motivation and better self-control.

— Kelly McGonigal

According to Buddhist teachings, self-compassion is essential to the path toward enlightenment and is seen as a way to alleviate suffering and promote happiness. When we are compassionate toward ourselves, we can accept ourselves as we are rather than constantly trying to improve or change ourselves. When we accept things as they are, we can find satisfaction and serenity in the present moment instead of becoming entangled in a cycle of pain and sorrow.

Self-compassion refers to the act of being kind and understanding toward oneself during difficult times, rather than being overly critical or judgmental. It involves treating ourselves with the same compassion and understanding that we would offer to a friend or loved one. Additionally, self-compassion is seen as a way to develop wisdom and understanding. We can see things more clearly and recognize the interconnectedness of all things and beings; this understanding leads to a greater sense of compassion for the world around us.

Empathy and Compassion

Empathy and self-compassion are the foundations of emotional intelligence, and when we can master them, we can genuinely thrive both personally and professionally. Empathy is the ability to understand and share the feelings of another person. It involves being able to perceive and respond to the emotional states of others accurately, or being able "to put ourselves in another's shoes."

Compassion involves not only understanding another person's feelings but also feeling motivated to help them somehow. It consists of the desire to alleviate suffering and offer comfort and support.

Empathy and compassion allow us to connect with others, understand their feelings, and accept our own emotions. When we can empathize with others, we build stronger relationships and create a more compassionate society.

It is possible to have empathy without feeling compassion, and vice versa. Someone empathetic may be able to understand and appreciate another person's feelings, but may not feel motivated to help them in any way. On the other hand, compassionate people may strongly desire to help others, even if they do not fully understand or share their feelings.

Turning compassion toward yourself involves taking a (pro)active approach to addressing and improving your own struggles. When we can practice self-compassion, we build inner strength and resilience, allowing us to navigate life's challenges with grace and understanding.

The Myths of Self-Compassion

Unfortunately, some common misconceptions about self-compassion discourage people from learning more about it. These misconceptions range from thinking self-compassion is the same as self-pity or laziness to believing it's not as important as self-esteem. We can take the first step toward developing self-compassion by recognizing and refuting these myths and misconceptions.

Myth: Self-compassion is selfish.

Fact: Self-compassion is the opposite of selfishness, and it involves acknowledging and accepting our own suffering, as well as the suffering of others. By being kind and understanding toward ourselves, we can be more present and available to support others.

Myth: Self-compassion is a sign of weakness.

Fact: Self-compassion is actually a sign of strength. It requires much courage to be honest with ourselves about our flaws and weaknesses.

Myth: Self-compassion is the same as self-indulgence.

Fact: Self-compassion is about finding balance. It involves taking care of ourselves and meeting our own needs; it does not mean indulging in unhealthy behaviors or neglecting our responsibilities.

Myth: Self-compassion is the same as self-pity.

Fact: Self-compassion involves acknowledging and accepting our own suffering, while self-pity involves dwelling on our suffering and feeling sorry for ourselves.

Myth: Self-compassion is easy.

Fact: Practicing self-compassion can be difficult, especially if we are used to being hard on ourselves. It requires acknowledging and accepting our flaws and weaknesses, which can be very challenging.

Myth: Self-compassion is the same as self-esteem.

Fact: While self-compassion and self-esteem are related, they are very different. Self-compassion is about treating oneself with kindness and understanding, even in difficult situations, while self-esteem is about valuing and approving ourselves. It says more about how much we think we are worth and how much we like ourselves.

Myth: Self-compassion is only for people with low self-esteem.

Fact: Self-compassion can be beneficial for people with all levels of self-esteem. It can help people with low self-esteem to feel more worthy and accepted, and it can help people with high self-esteem to be more realistic and balanced in their self-evaluations.

Myth: Self-compassion is only for people who are struggling.

Fact: While self-compassion can be especially helpful for people struggling with difficult emotions or challenges, it is not only for those struggling. Everyone can benefit from self-compassion, as it can help us feel more grounded, connected, and satisfied with our lives.

Now let's dive a little deeper into some of these misconceptions.

The Pursuit of High Self-Esteem

It's been drilled into our heads that having high self-esteem is crucial to happiness and success. But is it really that simple? Recent studies show that this constant need to view ourselves positively is backfiring on us.

Promoting high self-esteem has been trending and immensely popular for many years, with countless media outlets advocating it. However, studies reveal that pursuing high self-esteem can actually lead to an inflated sense of self-importance and a lack of empathy for others.

In a society where being average is seen as a failure, many people try to make themselves appear better than others, leading to increased levels of narcissism. In the past 20 years, this has become a serious issue, with 65% of college students displaying higher levels of narcissism than previous generations. This constant need to feel superior can lead to feelings of loneliness and disconnection.

One of the most common misconceptions about self-compassion is that it is the same as self-esteem. Although the two concepts are sometimes intertwined, they are very different. Self-compassion is a form of self-acceptance that does not depend on a person's performance or achievements and shifts the focus from trying to be perfect to simply being content with yourself.

Self-esteem is often based on external validation and comparison to others rather than an internal sense of self-worth. When our self-worth becomes too tied to meeting other people's expectations or standards, it can lead to a constant need for validation and a fear of failure. Additionally, high self-esteem doesn't always translate to positive self-regard and doesn't protect against negative emotions, such as shame and self-doubt. It may also cause or exacerbate feelings of isolation, whereas self-compassion helps individuals to see themselves more positively and as part of a collective, resulting in a stronger sense of belonging.

It's time to shift our focus from self-esteem to self-compassion. Instead of constantly criticizing ourselves for not being enough, we can fully embrace and accept ourselves for who we are in this very moment. Let's strive for a world where you wake up every morning and look in the mirror with nothing but love and appreciation for the person staring back at you. No more negative self-talk or harsh criticisms. Just pure, unconditional acceptance.

Shaking False Beliefs

Self-pity and self-indulgence often keep us from achieving our goals and living our best lives. We feel sorry for ourselves because of our perceived failures or setbacks and fear we might become lazy when we're 'too soft' on ourselves. However, it's important to note that self-pity and self-indulgence are very different from being self-compassionate.

The entanglement of self-pity

Self-pity is a trap that can easily ensnare individuals, causing them to become consumed with their struggles and problems, unable to see that others are also struggling and experiencing difficulties. It's a state of mind that leads us to feelings of isolation and disconnection from others. People who fall into this trap often exaggerate their sorrow and become fixated on their own pain, unable to empathize with others.

On the other hand, self-kindness offers a powerful antidote to these negative emotions by helping individuals recognize the shared humanity in their pain. It enables them to see their own experiences in the context of the larger human experience and to understand that they are not alone in their pain. It can help them avoid the tendency to be overly dramatic and melodramatic about their bad luck and misfortunes.

Self-pity can make it hard to gain distance from your predicament and see things more clearly. It facilitates getting trapped in a bubble, which makes it difficult to see the bigger picture. Practicing self-compassion, however, allows you to step back and view yourself with the same empathy and understanding as an objective third party. This perspective allows you to gain a broader understanding of your situation and helps you find a way to move forward.

The Fine Line of Self-indulgence

Many of us find it challenging to be compassionate toward ourselves because we fear that we might let ourselves off the hook too much. We think being kind to ourselves is the same as indulging in unhealthy habits, like eating junk food, sleeping late, and watching too much TV. But that's not proper self-care; that's self-indulgence.

Taking care of ourselves and achieving lasting enjoyment usually entails a certain level of discomfort. Maintaining good health, developing new skills, and pursuing meaningful experiences often involves pushing ourselves out of our comfort zones, which forces us to face challenges and obstacles. Confronting these difficulties and overcoming them will allow us to grow and find a deeper sense of fulfillment and satisfaction.

Real self-compassion is about striving for long-term wellness. Giving in to instant pleasure can often be detrimental to our overall health, but genuine self-compassion is about making choices that will lead to sustainable vitality and happiness.

Chapter Takeaways

- Self-compassion is a concept borrowed from Buddhism aimed at alleviating suffering.
- Treating oneself the same kindness we would have for a best friend is at the heart of self-compassion.
- Empathy and compassion allow us to connect with others and ourselves deeply.

- There are a lot of myths and misconceptions about self-compassion that prevent us from fully reaping its benefits.
- To truly understand the concept of self-compassion, we must learn its difference from self-esteem, self-pity, and self-indulgence.

2. The Benefits of Self-Compassion

Practice self-compassion. Talk to and be your best, kind, compassionate, caring friend.

— Kristin Neff

Self-compassion is one of the most potent sources of resilience. It has many positive effects, such as lowering levels of loneliness, improving concentration, and lessening the tendency to "project" your feelings onto others. It is the antidote to self-attacking and has proven to conquer "the inner critic." It helps us tone down our self-flagellating attitudes, behaviors, and feelings that steal away our confidence and peace of mind and set off our unhealthy coping mechanisms.

By learning to be kind to ourselves, we can turn off our brain's threat system and instead turn toward our "safety/soothing system," allowing us to face our feelings head-on and react more efficiently to the trials of daily life.

Advantages of Self-Compassion

Self-compassion is a strong predictor of happiness; people who master it tend to be less depressed, less nervous, and less prone to experiencing excessive shame (or even suicide ideation). Practicing it drastically improves emotional well-being, builds a stronger sense of self-worth, develops resilience, and improves our relationships and physical health.

Let's get straight to it and have a deeper look at the many benefits of self-compassion:

Improving emotional well-being: Self-compassion has been shown to reduce symptoms of depression, anxiety, and stress. Instead of criticizing yourself or dwelling on negative thoughts, you'll learn to understand and accept your flaws and limitations, allowing you to better cope with difficult emotions like shame and guilt.

Cultivating self-kindness allows us to accept our humanity and to be more understanding and accepting of ourselves, warts and all. Instead of weakening ourselves with self-criticism and doubt, we can build ourselves up with self-compassion.

Think of it like going on an adventurous journey. You set out with high hopes and big dreams but encounter obstacles and setbacks along the way. Instead of giving up, self-compassion helps you to see these challenges as opportunities for growth and development. It's like having a trusty companion by your side, encouraging you to keep going and to take care of yourself along the way.

Enhancing self-worth: Self-compassion helps individuals to develop a more stable and healthy sense of self-worth. Unlike self-esteem, which is based on external validation, self-compassion is an unconditional form of self-acceptance. It allows you to fully accept yourself as you are, which leads to a more stable and robust sense of self-worth.

Self-worth that is solely based on having high self-esteem is predicated on competition with others and excelling at something to feel good about yourself. It is based on success and makes it easy to give up on yourself when you fail. Basing your self-worth on self-compassion means treating yourself with kindness, understanding, and acceptance, rather than constantly seeking external validation. It involves recognizing and accepting your own flaws, failures, and imperfections, while also acknowledging and embracing your strengths, accomplishments, and successes. By approaching yourself with self-compassion, you can develop a healthier, more fulfilling sense of self-worth and emotional well-being.

Facilitating personal growth: Self-compassion allows you to acknowledge your flaws and mistakes without feeling guilty or ashamed. People who are very hard on themselves may find it hard to take risks because they fear disappointment or failure. When you have less of a fear of failure, you are more willing to venture out into the unknown. You create a safe space for yourself to learn from mishaps and examine yourself lovingly, leading to healthy personal growth.

Self-compassion fosters personal growth by encouraging introspection and improving self-awareness. By attentively observing your emotions and thoughts, you gain a deeper insight into your priorities, needs, and values. This leads to a better understanding of yourself and helps you see the steps you need to take to reach your goals.

Improving relationships: Self-compassion will also have a positive impact on your relationships. It will help you to be more empathetic and understanding, and less critical and judgmental, toward others.

When it comes to relationships, it's important to remember that we can only be as kind and patient to others as we are to ourselves. That's where self-compassion comes in. Practicing self-empathy can help us to become better partners, friends, family members, colleagues, bosses, and parents. It's like a secret recipe for success in our relationships.

Imagine being more at ease with yourself, like slipping into your favorite pair of jeans. It's that comfortable, confident feeling that makes it easier to connect with others. By learning to be more self-compassionate, you'll become less self-centered and develop your capacity for empathy.

Promoting resilience: Self-compassion helps you to see your problems and difficulties from a broader perspective, which can help you to feel less overwhelmed and more resilient in the face of adversity. When you learn to be more self-compassionate, you are more likely to view challenges as opportunities for growth and development rather than overwhelming obstacles.

When failures don't seem so catastrophic and self-criticism fades into the background, you'll have more time to find pleasure in life. Mistakes and failures can be seen as learning opportunities rather than reflections of our character, which can lead to a healthier self-image and more positive outlook on life. Spending less time ruminating on past failures and failings leaves more time for the things and people you truly value.

Improving physical health: Self-compassion has been linked to a reduction in anxiety and stress on a physiological level. Self-criticism and self-judgment can trigger a "threat state," where the limbic system is heightened, and your "fight or flight" response is initiated. Constant exposure to this state has been linked to anxiety and depression.

Perhaps you have experienced the calming effect of a friend's encouraging words or comforting touch in times of hardship. We share that beautiful effect with ourselves when we show affection and love. The hormone oxytocin is released in response to giving and receiving compassion, enhancing feelings of security, trust, and calmness.

Self-compassion also helps us be more mindful of our well-being; it's like having a GPS for the body and soul. From regular exercise and healthy eating to avoiding harmful habits like smoking and excessive drinking, self-compassion empowers us to make choices consistent with our long-term health.

Instead of focusing on short-term pleasure, we can learn to shift toward a long-term perspective on our physical and mental wellness. We invest more time and energy into making decisions that will benefit us and our future selves.

Chapter Takeaways

- Self-compassion is a highly effective means of coping in healthier ways.
- Self-compassion is a powerful tool that can help individuals to improve their emotional well-being, build a stronger sense of self-worth, develop resilience, and improve their relationships and physical health.
- Having greater self-compassion makes you more tenacious and speeds up your recovery after experiencing negative emotions like shame, guilt, or anger.

3. Embracing your Inner-Critic

Too many people overvalue what they are not and undervalue what they are.

— Malcolm S. Forbes

I know how challenging it can be to show yourself kindness, trust me. Activating the calming system can be a unique experience that may provoke resistance and complicated feelings. This is because it is very different from the more familiar threat-driven cycle many people are accustomed to. When first learning to practice self-compassion, it is common to experience an increase in negative thoughts. Do any of the following thoughts sound familiar to you:

"I don't have time for self-compassion. I need to focus on getting things done."

"Being too understanding toward myself means I'm not holding myself accountable."

"I don't deserve a break. I should just tough it out."

"If I'm not criticizing myself, I'll never improve."

"Being nicer to myself means I'm not taking things seriously."

"If I'm too kind to myself, I'll become a pushover, and people will walk all over me."

We all have those negative thoughts that creep into our minds and make us doubt ourselves. They tell us we're not good enough, that our goals are unattainable, and that our accomplishments don't matter. These thoughts might greet us in the morning as we look in the mirror, telling us how unattractive we are and how we're not good enough. They might pop up at work, telling us that we're not capable of handling the pressure and that we're invisible to others. And they might even influence our closest relationships, making us question whether we're truly loved and if our relationships will last. But here's the thing: these thoughts don't define us. We are so much more than the negative voices in our heads.

When it comes to practicing self-compassion, there may be times when it feels like you're climbing a mountain of insurmountable negative thoughts and feelings. But fear not; several strategies can help you overcome these barriers when learning to be kinder to yourself.

Cultivating Empathy and Compassion

One approach is to start by cultivating empathy for others and gradually working your way toward being more compassionate to yourself. It may be easier to show compassion for others before turning that emotion inward. Think of it like a warm-up before a big game. This tactic is like a stepping stone that helps you ease into feeling kindness toward yourself, transforming your inner critic into an inner friend.

Exercise

1. Start by setting aside some quiet time for yourself. Find a comfortable place where you can sit undisturbed for a few minutes.
2. Close your eyes and slowly try to let go of any thoughts or distractions by focusing on your breath. Take your time and keep your attention on breathing in and breathing out.
3. Now, bring to mind someone you care about. It could be a friend, family member, or even someone you don't know personally but admire. Imagine this person in your mind and try to feel empathy for them. Imagine what they might be going through, what they might be feeling, and what they might need.
4. As you focus on this person, feel compassion for them. Imagine yourself sending them love and support. Try to feel the warmth and kindness in your heart as you think of them. Focus on your bodily sensations. Where do you feel the warmth and kindness?
5. Once you have practiced empathy and compassion for someone else, bring your focus back to yourself. Remember that you are also human and have struggles and difficulties. Recognize your shared humanity with others.
6. As you focus on yourself, try to extend the same compassion and understanding to yourself that

you were feeling for the person you were thinking of earlier. Focus on the bodily sensations you felt earlier and try to direct them toward yourself. Feel the warmth and kindness in your heart as you think of yourself.

7. Notice when you're being self-critical and try to reframe those thoughts in a more compassionate way. Challenge them by asking yourself where they're coming from and if they're true. Are they based on facts or emotions?

8. Take a moment to breathe deeply and release any tension you might be holding in your body. Allow yourself to let go of any distractions or worries and fully immerse yourself in the present moment. If it feels good, you can even release a sigh to help release any pent-up emotions. Take your time and allow yourself to relax and be in the present moment.

Imagining a Loved One's Perspective

Another approach is to put yourself in the shoes of a loved one. Imagine how they would perceive you and your situation. This can be much more effective than trying to generate feelings of self-compassion on your own. You can gain a new perspective on your situation and self-worth by seeing things differently.

Think about it, when you're feeling down, it's easy to get stuck in your head, and it can be hard to see the good in yourself. But, when you imagine how a loved one would perceive you, their love and concern for you can be a powerful reminder that you are worthy of kindness and compassion.

Exercise

1. Start by setting aside some quiet time for yourself. Find a comfortable place where you can sit undisturbed for a few minutes.
2. Close your eyes and focus on your breath. Take a few deep breaths in and out, and try to let go of any thoughts or distractions.
3. Bring to mind someone you love and trust. Imagine this person standing in front of you and try to picture their face clearly.
4. Imagine that you are explaining your current situation to this person and how you are feeling about it. Try to be as honest and open as possible.
5. Now, imagine how this person would respond to you. Feel their love and concern for you. Try to feel it in your body; in your heart. Imagine what they would say to you and how they would comfort you.
6. Take a moment to reflect on their response and how it makes you feel. Notice the warmth and kindness you feel. And let this feeling vibrate throughout your whole body.

Getting to the Root

You can get past your resistance to self-compassion if you take a good, hard look at the things that might be standing in the way. Self-compassion can be challenging to cultivate because of deeply ingrained, often learned, attitudes and emotions. In today's culture, where striving for perfection is highly valued, making a mistake may seem unacceptable. Complicating factors in relationships and interpersonal traumas can also teach us unconsciously that we aren't worthy of kindness and that love puts us in harm's way.

Beginning a self-compassion practice can feel strange initially, but that doesn't imply it's not doable. It's not like we're picking up an entirely new talent here. It eventually becomes second nature to treat ourselves like we would a trusted friend. Our natural instinct to fight or flee the situation makes us feel uneasy. When we make a mistake, our bodies react similarly under intense stress. We wage war on ourselves by verbally assaulting and humiliating ourselves to maintain some semblance of self-discipline or power. Or, we may become paralyzed, sinking into guilt and isolation.

Understanding the source of your negative thoughts and feelings can help you to take control and make them more manageable. It's essential to question the validity of these thoughts and feelings and to make an effort to change or challenge them.

By understanding the underlying causes of your negative thoughts and feelings, you can work toward making them more pliable. Thus, it will be easier for you to practice self-compassion.

Exercise

1. Find a comfortable place where you can sit in silence for a few minutes. It could be your living room, backyard, or car. Just make sure you won't be interrupted.

2. Now, close your eyes and focus on your breath. Take a few deep breaths in and out, and try to let go of any thoughts or distractions. Let yourself relax and release any tension in your body.

3. Once you feel calm and centered, bring to mind a specific negative thought or feeling that prevents you from practicing self-compassion. It could be a thought such as "I'm not good enough", "This is stupid" or "I don't know if I can do this." Spend a few moments focusing on that thought or feeling and let yourself feel it fully.

4. Next, take a moment to examine where this thought or feeling came from. Ask yourself: "Is this thought or feeling truly my own, or are there external factors influencing it?" "Can I find ways to challenge or change this negative thought or feeling?" These questions are designed to help you understand the validity of your thoughts and feelings. It's important to realize that just because you have a thought doesn't mean you have to believe it or think it's true. Similarly, just because you have a feeling doesn't mean you have to act on it. The exercise helps you learn to challenge negative thoughts and manage complicated feelings.

5. Instead of trying to silence your thoughts or push your negative feelings away, try to accept and be with them. This is an integral part of self-compassion. Imagine yourself offering comfort to a loved one who is going through a difficult time. You wouldn't try to change their thoughts or feelings; you would simply be there for them and offer your support. The same applies to yourself.

Accepting and being with your negative thoughts
and feelings is not trying to change anything;
you're simply being present and allowing yourself
to feel and process whatever you're experiencing.

It can be easy to get caught up in negative thoughts and
feelings that make us feel like we are not good enough. By
understanding the origins of our inner critic and learning to
be more compassionate toward ourselves, we can overcome
these barriers and learn to practice self-compassion more
effectively. Remember, self-compassion is not about
ignoring or pushing away negative thoughts or feelings, but
rather, it's about understanding and accepting them.

Chapter Takeaways

- When you first start experiencing your own
  kindness, you may feel resistance and experience
  an increase in negative thoughts.
- Easing into self-compassion by first focusing on the
  needs of others before directing that feeling
  toward oneself may be more manageable.
- By considering how a loved one would perceive
  you, you can shift your focus away from your
  perspective and gain a fresh and less biased
  viewpoint on your situation.
- By understanding and accepting negative thoughts
  and feelings, we can overcome these barriers and
  learn to be kinder to ourselves.

4. Developing Loving-Kindness

The most powerful relationship you will ever have is with yourself.

— Steve Maraboli

Loving-kindness, also known as "metta" in Buddhism, is a powerful practice used for centuries to help individuals develop feelings of love and compassion toward themselves and others. It's a technique passed down from ancient Eastern spiritual traditions but has recently been adapted and studied in modern Western psychology. The purpose of this practice is to help us overcome the natural tendency to focus on our suffering and the suffering of those close to us and, instead, to open our hearts and develop a sense of inter-connectedness with all beings.

Imagine being able to reduce stress, anxiety, and depression just by taking a few minutes each day to focus on love and compassion. That's the beauty of a loving-kindness meditation. Research has proven that regularly practicing this technique leads to many benefits, including lower levels of anxiety, stress, and depression.

Getting caught up in our problems and becoming trapped in a cycle of negative thoughts and feelings is easy nowadays. Loving-kindness meditation offers a way to break free from this cycle and develop a more compassionate and understanding perspective toward ourselves and others. It's an essential practice for anyone looking to improve their overall well-being. So, whether you want to reduce stress, improve your relationships, or feel more connected to the world around you, give loving-kindness a try and experience the benefits for yourself.

Loving-Kindness Meditation

The Loving-kindness meditation is a powerful practice that helps us tap into our innate capacity for compassion and kindness. It's important to remember that the words we use during the meditation are just tools, and the true focus should be on the feelings they induce. As we practice, the novelty of the words may start to fade, and that's okay. It's natural for our minds to wander, and the key is to bring our attention back to the emotion of loving-kindness.

This practice might sometimes feel awkward or frustrating (it's not uncommon for our minds to bring up negative emotions like anger or annoyance), but instead of getting caught up in these feelings, try to be gentle and compassionate with yourself. Accept whatever arises, and approach it with warmth and openness rather than judgment or shame.

It's also important to remember that this is not a one-time meditation, it takes time and practice to see the benefits, and the journey is what makes it all worth it.

Preparation

The first step in preparing for a loving-kindness meditation is to get comfortable. Sit with your feet flat on the floor, legs uncrossed, and back straight. Place your hands on your lap and take a moment to feel the connection of your body with the chair and the floor. Make yourself feel completely at ease.

Close your eyes if it feels comfortable. If it doesn't, you can gaze into your lap. Take a moment to observe your current state of sitting. It's like being a detective, investigating the present moment with curiosity.

As you tune in to your physical self and your breath, allow yourself to be present and aware, ready to accept whatever comes your way. You're going to be a true friend who is there for you every step of the way.

Calm your breathing and let go of any judgments or criticism. Just be. Take note of the inflow and outflow of your breath, like the tide coming in and going out. Feel the air passing through your nostrils and watch your chest rise and fall.

Now you're all set for your loving-kindness meditation journey, ready to explore the depths of compassion and kindness within yourself. So, take a deep breath, relax and let's begin.

Mindful attention

Once you're comfortable and in a relaxed state, it's time to focus your attention on your chest, close to your heart. This is where the magic happens. As you repeat to yourself in a soft and quiet voice, "Love. I pray that my heart will be filled with love," take a moment to feel the reverberation of the words in your chest.

Now, imagine someone or something you feel intense love and care for. It could be a loved one, a cherished pet, a favorite character from a book or show, or even a tree in your backyard.

Think about the warmth and happiness this person or thing brings you. Imagine the love and care radiating out of your chest and enveloping them.

Don't worry if you're unable to visualize or simply don't want to, it's ok, the feelings of love and kindness are the most important.

As you continue to repeat the phrase, "Love. I pray that my heart will be filled with love," allow yourself to fully immerse in the feeling of love and let it fill your heart and radiate throughout your body. It's like taking a warm bath for the soul.

This is a simple but powerful way to cultivate a feeling of loving-kindness toward yourself and others. Take a deep breath, relax, and let the love flow.

The cultivation of loving-kindness

As you focus on your heart, let a wave of compassion, kindness, and warmth wash over your entire being. Relax into the experience of these emotions. Now whisper to yourself slowly and repeatedly:

- May I always be brimming with loving kindness.
- May I be protected from all harm, both internal and external.
- May I be happy and contented.
- May all be well with my mind and body.
- May I find comfort and joy.
- May I forever rest in tranquility.

It may seem strange to speak kindly to yourself or even entertain such thoughts. Just keep repeating the sentences until you notice everything dissolving into the sensation of feeling safe and protected in this moment, the feeling of being content and happy in this moment, and the feeling of being complete in this moment.

Self-compassion is a practice not everyone feels immediately comfortable with. If you're having trouble, don't worry. It's normal, and it may take some time to get into the habit of doing this. So don't rush it; take your time.

Practicing kindness toward a loved one

Now think of someone you admire, appreciate, and respect, or perhaps someone who cares a great deal about you and only wants the best for you. It can be someone from the past or present, alive or who is no longer with us.

Imagine this person, and send them your best wishes. For example:

- I hope that you are protected from harm, both within and without.

- I hope that you are feeling good in both body and mind.
- I hope that you find peace and joy in life.

You may not even need words if you have a deep wellspring of compassion. This is your time for reflection, so feel free to adjust the practice as necessary.

Remember, sending love and kindness with an open heart is the most important thing. It's a small but powerful gesture of love.

Repeat the process with someone else in mind who is very important to you, for example your significant other. It's not about how many people you send loving-kindness to, but about the intensity, you send it with.

Extending kindness to a person who has no particular bias

Now, do the same thing with someone you don't know very well but don't dislike either. This could be a stranger you've seen on the street, on the bus, or in the hallway at work. Wish them well by sending these loving sentiments:

- I wish you to be brimming with loving kindness.
- I hope you are protected from harm, both within and without.
- I hope that you are feeling good in both body and mind.
- I hope that you find peace and joy in life.
- My wish is that you find rest and tranquility.

Sometimes, people may feel like they've lost touch with their capacity for kindness. But don't worry; it's never too late to reconnect with those feelings and start caring again. There's no need to rush; take your time cultivating a high-quality emotional response.

Extending compassion to someone who has upset or irritated you

Now, think of someone you've disagreed with or who has slightly annoyed you; it could be a colleague at work or a driver who cut you off on the road.

It's natural to have negative feelings toward someone who has irritated you but instead of holding on to those negative emotions, take this moment to extend compassion and kindness toward them.

It's not about agreeing with someone's behavior; it's about being able to treat them with respect and empathy.

Extending loving kindness to someone who has wronged you

As you focus on your heart area, think of someone who has wronged you. It could be someone who hurt you emotionally, betrayed your trust, or caused you pain in any way.

This might be the hardest part of this meditation, so be extra kind to yourself. Showing empathy for someone who has wronged us can be incredibly difficult. It's natural to feel anger and resentment toward the person who has hurt us, but holding on to these emotions can be a heavy burden to carry. It can weigh us down and prevent us from moving forward in our lives.

It's important to remember that empathy is not the same as forgiveness. Empathy means understanding and being able to relate to the feelings and experiences of another person. It doesn't mean that we excuse or justify their actions. However, by showing empathy, we can begin to understand why they might have acted the way they did and begin to let go of our anger and resentment towards them.

Now take this moment to extend compassion and kindness toward them.

Whisper to yourself slowly and repeatedly, "I wish you are protected from harm, both from inside and out", "I hope you feel good in body and mind", "I wish you find peace and joy in life", "I hope you find rest and tranquility."

Take a deep breath, relax and let the wave of compassion and love wash over this person. I know it's not easy, but showing compassion is a powerful tool that helps us heal and move on. It takes courage and self-awareness and is worth the effort in the end.

Now take a moment to recognize and appreciate what you have just done. Give yourself recognition for the incredible effort you made. Allow yourself to feel proud and give yourself the support and encouragement you need in this moment.

Putting out into the world a feeling of unconditional love

Now, expand your act of kindness outward to everyone and everything on Earth and beyond. Imagine a world filled with love and kindness, where everyone is protected, happy, and at peace.

It's like sending a love letter to the entire world, wishing everyone all the love, protection, and well-being. It's a way of spreading love and kindness to every corner of the world.

Practicing kindness and self-love toward oneself

Return your focus to yourself and allow loving kindness to fill your entire being. Breathe in peace and exhale peace. Be at peace with yourself and the world. Allow these emotions to permeate you while you softly and silently repeat to yourself:

- May I always be brimming with loving kindness.
- May I be protected from all dangers, both internal and external.
- May I be well in mind and body.
- May I find comfort and joy.
- May I forever rest in tranquility.

Finishing up

As you reach the end of your meditation practice, allow the warm fuzzies and feelings of love and kindness to fade away in their own time. Take a moment to come back to your breath, noticing the rise and fall of your chest and the sensation of the air moving in and out of your nostrils.

Take stock of your seating position, feeling the connection between your body and the chair, and the connection between your feet and the ground.

Notice the sounds around you, the gentle hum of traffic or birds chirping outside, and the natural ambiance of the present moment.

Take in the beautiful orange-brown hue of light you see against your eyelids, and when you're ready, gently open your eyes and focus on the present.

It's like coming back from a magical love-filled journey, feeling refreshed and rejuvenated, ready to take on the world with a heart filled with love and compassion.

Chapter Takeaways

- The practice of "loving-kindness" can help reduce our connection to painful mental states, allowing us to better weather their storms without being entirely overwhelmed.
- Loving-kindness involves showing love to yourself, people you love and admire, and even those who have annoyed or hurt you.

5. The Map of Self-Compassion

You've criticized yourself for years, and it hasn't worked. Try approving of yourself and see what happens.

— Louise L. Hay

This chapter is designed to be a resource that you can come back to time and time again as you work to cultivate self-compassion in your life. The exercises and meditations included are meant to help you explore and strengthen your ability to be kind and understanding toward yourself. Whether you're new to self-compassion or looking for ways to deepen your existing practice, you'll find something that resonates with you here.

Take your time, explore the different exercises and meditations, and find the ones that work for you. Remember, self-compassion is a journey, not a destination, and with each step you take, you're one step closer to a more compassionate and kinder relationship with yourself.

Compassionate Body Scan

This exercise will focus on honing our physical selves through self-care. Too often, we neglect our bodies and only pay attention to them when they are in pain. Instead of wanting to impress others, self-care is about ensuring that we stay well and recognize the significance of our bodies' efforts on our behalf. Let's take a moment to appreciate the beautiful capabilities that our bodies possess and work on nurturing and valuing them. Let's begin.

Bring your attention to your current sitting position and make any necessary adjustments to focus completely on what's being said during the next few moments. Drop whatever has been stressing you out, worrying you, or otherwise weighing you down. Put both feet flat on the floor, keep your back straight but not rigid, loosen up your shoulders and facial muscles, and put your hands on your thighs or lap. You can close your eyes slowly.

Pause

It's easy to let our minds wander and leave our bodies behind. Mindful centering aims to bring us and our bodies back to the present moment. Take a few deep breaths to align your attention and body. Inhale through your nose, and exhale through your mouth, letting out a slow and leisurely breath. Repeat this process a few more times. As you release your breath, pay attention to how your body responds. This simple yet powerful practice brings harmony between your mind and body.

Pause

Now, observe the natural rhythm of your inhalations and exhalations as you let your breath move at its own rate. Take a few moments to focus on how it feels to breathe.

Short pause

It's natural for your mind to wander during this practice. If your thoughts stray, don't worry, it's normal. Without judgment, acknowledge the distraction and release it. Bring your focus back to your breath and continue with the practice. Remember, it's not about perfection but about being mindful and present in the moment.

Short pause

Let's look into your internal experiences now. Focus on the sensations you're currently experiencing. Take a walk through your body, starting at the top of your head and working your way down. As you scan through your body, take note of any areas that feel tense, relaxed, or neutral. For example, you may notice a tightness in your jaw or a knot in your shoulders or may notice a sense of calm in your chest or a feeling of lightness in your legs. Whatever you feel, don't try to change it, simply acknowledge it.

Short pause

Now, take a moment to evaluate your current mental state. Notice when you become aware of a thought and label it as "thinking." After you have labeled the thought, come back to your breathing.

Short pause

Get in touch with your feelings now. Don't worry about trying to interpret the origin of your feelings; simply say the word "feeling" as you're experiencing them and return to your breathing. Keep in mind that you aren't looking for how much or how little you can observe. The point is to pay attention to your internal experiences without judgment.

Short pause

Now let's focus on taking care of our physical health. We often only pay attention to our bodies when they are in pain instead of valuing and nurturing them when they are well. We should appreciate the amazing things our bodies can do for us and strive to improve our ability to care for ourselves. Let's give some thought to the incredible capabilities that our bodies currently possess and work on improving our ability to nurture and value them.

Pause

As you take your next breath, deliberately focus on your face—experiment with relaxing your facial muscles, starting with your eyebrows and jaw. Our heads are incredibly complex and powerful, allowing us to communicate, express emotions, eat, see, smell, hear, think, and taste. Take a moment to appreciate the hard work your facial muscles put in every day and allow them to rest and recover.

Short pause

Now, bring your attention to your neck and shoulders. If you feel any tension, try to release it with your next exhale. Our necks and shoulders often bear the weight of carrying heavy objects, and the strain of working at a computer and stress from our daily lives can also manifest as pain in these areas. Show gratitude and care for your neck and shoulders by taking a few deep breaths and letting go of any tension.

Short pause

Bring your focus to the chest area now. Notice how your chest rises and falls with each breath. Try listening to the sound of your heartbeat. The lungs and heart are vital for our energy system as they bring in oxygen and distribute it throughout the body. It is also the area where deep emotions such as happiness, sadness, joy, and grief originate. Take a moment to focus on this area of your body and pay attention to any sensations you may be experiencing.

Short pause

Bring your attention to your belly button now. Notice how your stomach moves with each breath. Feel your lower back move with each inhale and exhale. We often take for granted the work our stomachs do for us. Think about how your stomach processes food and provides energy for the rest of your body. Take a moment to appreciate and thank your stomach for all its hard work.

Short pause

Focus on your limbs now. How do your arms & hands feel? Are they cold, warm, or tired? Reflect on their sensations. Relax them and appreciate their capabilities. Think about the many times you use them during the day. Imagine how different your life would be without the ability to use your hands and arms.

Short pause

Take a deep, cleansing breath and direct your attention to your legs. Become aware of any sensations you might be feeling in your legs at this moment. Is there any tightness, discomfort, or fatigue?

Recognize the amazing things your legs are doing for you every single day. They have carried you through every step of your life's journey, supporting you and allowing you to move, explore, and experience the world around you.

Acknowledge the importance of taking care of your legs to ensure they are in top condition.

Short pause

Let's bring our attention to solely our feet. Notice where they make contact with the floor. Imagine breathing directly into your toes, and visualize yourself relaxing and massaging your feet with each exhale. Consider the feeling of taking responsibility for your own foot care. Your feet are the foundation of your body, and they work tirelessly to support you and the rest of your body every day.

Short pause

Take a deep breath and let it fill you up from head to toe; repeat this several times. Allow the air to reach every part of your body. Imagine it as an inward hug that you are giving yourself. Acknowledge and celebrate your body and all its features as you go through your day. Pay attention to how your body works as you use your hands to write or your feet to walk. Make a point to appreciate and be grateful for your physical self throughout the day.

Pause

When you are ready, slowly open your eyes. Take your time, and don't rush. Gradually start moving your fingers and toes, then your whole body, stretching gently and comfortably. Enjoy this wonderful feeling.

Self-Acceptance

In this meditation, we will work on self-acceptance and cultivating love and compassion for ourselves. We will explore how we can release negative thoughts or judgments about ourselves and learn to embrace our unique qualities and imperfections. Remember, self-acceptance is a journey and not a destination. Take a deep breath, and let's start.

1. First things first, let's get comfortable! Plant your feet firmly on the ground, and let your arms hang naturally by your sides. Place your hands on your lap, and bring your shoulder blades together. Lower your chin, so it's level with the floor, and raise your head so the crown faces upward. Take a moment to adjust your jaw and stomach for maximum comfort.

2. Now that you're settled, take a moment to appreciate the feeling of stillness. Take in the sensation of sitting in this thoughtful position at this precise time in this exact location. Give yourself a warm welcome to your practice, and acknowledge your desire to be here for yourself.

3. Next, let's focus on our breath. Pay attention to the sensation of the air entering and leaving your lungs. There's no need to control or alter your breath; just let it be as it is. Concentrate on your in and out breaths.

4. As you breathe, pay attention to where the sensation of breathing lands. You might feel the air

entering and leaving your nose or the sensation of your chest and ribs expanding and contracting. Maybe you'll notice your stomach rising and falling. Just relax and focus on the ins and outs of your breath for a while.

5. As you focus on your breath, you may find random thoughts pop into your head. Don't worry, this is normal! Instead of trying to shut them out, let your thoughts pass through your mind one at a time. Recognize that these thoughts are just thoughts, and they do not define you as a person. Observe your thoughts without judgment and without attachment.

6. As you continue to breathe and focus on your thoughts, pay attention to any emotions that may arise. Take deep breaths in and out, and accept your feelings exactly as they are. Remember, all feelings are valid and encouraged in this practice.

7. Imagine yourself surrounded by a warm and loving light. This light represents the love and acceptance that you have for yourself. As you continue to inhale, imagine that light growing brighter and brighter, filling your body and mind with a sense of self-love and acceptance.

8. Take a moment to focus on all the things you appreciate about yourself, your strengths, your kindness, your determination, your courage, your ability to learn, your ability to grow, etc.

9. Check in with your posture, and see if it has changed at all. Tune in with your body, notice any sensations, and adjust anything that feels uncomfortable.

10. As you come to the close of this practice, take three more deep breaths in and out. Be present for each and every one of them. Remember, you have access to this state of being at all times, within yourself.

11. When you're ready, slowly open your eyes and take in your immediate surroundings. As you go about your day, strive to be present and conscious in all of your interactions.

Resolving Emotional Wounds from The Past

In this meditation, we will explore how faith can help us heal from past emotional wounds and find peace in the present moment. We will focus on the power of forgiveness, gratitude, and trust and how these elements can support us in our journey toward emotional healing.

Pain and suffering can lead to significant growth and personal development. Through these difficult experiences, we can learn and understand ourselves more deeply. However, it is essential to maintain a sense of hope and optimism to navigate these challenging times effectively. We can work toward healing and finding new perspectives by aligning our hearts, minds, and actions. Keep in mind that adversity often leads to personal growth and development.

By the end of this meditation, you will have a deeper understanding of the restorative power of faith and how you can use it to resolve your own emotional wounds.

- Find a comfortable position and start by focusing on your breath. Take a moment to settle into your body and let go of any tension you may be holding.

- Bring to mind any emotional wounds you may be carrying with you. It can be memories or feelings of hurt, betrayal, or disappointment. Acknowledge and accept these emotions without judgment.
- Imagine that you are holding each of these wounds in your hands. See them as physical objects, and feel how heavy and burdensome they are.
- Take a deep breath and exhale away any negative emotions or bodily sensations that may not be serving you. Paying attention to your breath can bring a sense of calm and tranquility to your mind and body. Let your thoughts drift effortlessly along with each exhale.
- Now, let's focus on the power of forgiveness. Imagine that you can forgive the person or situation that caused these wounds and feel the weight of the wounds begin to lift as you forgive.
- Next, we will focus on gratitude. Imagine that you are grateful for the lessons and growth that came from these wounds. See yourself becoming stronger and more resilient due to what you have gone through.
- Finally, let's focus on trust. Imagine that you trust in a higher power, whether it be a god, the universe, or your own inner guidance, to lead you toward healing and peace. See yourself letting go of the wounds and trusting that you will be guided toward what is best for you.
- As you continue to focus on forgiveness, gratitude, and trust, feel the emotional wounds begin to fade away. Imagine that they are being replaced with light and peace. Take a moment to feel the peace and tranquility that comes with healing.

- Remember that healing is a process and the power of hope can help us through the difficult moments. Trust in yourself and the journey, and know that you are becoming stronger and more resilient with each step.
- When you are ready, take one more deep breath and open your eyes. Remember that the restorative power of faith is always available to you whenever you need it.

Cultivate Compassion

In this meditation, we will use the NEED technique to bring awareness to our thoughts, emotions, and physical sensations, as we focus on cultivating compassion toward ourselves and others. The NEED technique is a powerful tool to help us develop a deeper understanding of ourselves and the world around us by bringing awareness to our experiences in a non-judgmental way. During this meditation, we will use the four steps of Notice, Embrace, Examine, and Detach, to help us bring compassion to the present moment. Let's begin by finding a comfortable position, closing our eyes, and taking a deep breath.

Notice

As you take a deep breath, begin recognizing your thoughts, emotions, and physical sensations. Take a moment to acknowledge what is present in your mind and body.

You might notice your racing thoughts or a feeling of tightness in your chest. You may feel a knot in your stomach, or your shoulders may be tense. Whatever it is, observe it and acknowledge it. Like a detective on the case, you're gathering evidence of what's going on in your mind and body. By recognizing these thoughts, emotions, and physical sensations, we're setting the stage for the next steps of our meditation.

Embrace

The following minute will consist of taking a slow, deep breath and allowing yourself to be. As you exhale, imagine yourself blowing away any resistance to your thoughts, emotions, and physical sensations. It's like releasing a helium balloon into the sky, letting go of the string, and watching it float away.

Notice if there is any judgment or criticism you might have toward yourself or others. And let it be without trying to change or push it away. This step is all about embracing the present moment without trying to change anything.

Examine

Now take a closer look at your thoughts, emotions, and physical sensations. Observe them with curiosity and without judgment, like a scientist studying a specimen under a microscope. Ask yourself, what might be the underlying issue that is causing these thoughts, emotions, and sensations? It's like solving a puzzle, piecing together the clues to understand the bigger picture. This step is about understanding and gaining insight into your thoughts, emotions, and physical sensations.

At this point, we usually start to feel some strain. When we practice openness and curiosity with love, we can identify, grant permission, and inquire into the regions of our inner world that need care, cultivation, and nurturing, just like tending to a garden. We can reap a harvest of understanding and success by nurturing these parts of ourselves.

Detach

In this last step, we're going to detach from the experience by recognizing that it is not a part of the self but simply something that is happening in the present moment. Picture yourself stepping back and observing the experience from a distance, like watching a movie. You are a wise and loving observer who can see the situation clearly without getting caught up in it.

Try to bring an open heart and a sense of loving awareness without becoming too wrapped up in the situation. You want to prevent shifting into judgment and conviction, which will take you away from the disarming and curious state of mind that comes from simply sitting in natural awareness.

Take a deep breath and release all the tension from your body as you exhale. Imagine yourself freeing all the tension from your body like a balloon deflating. Take a moment to be with yourself and your compassionate intentions. Imagine yourself surrounded by a warm and loving energy and a sense of compassion. Allow this compassion to radiate outwards, enveloping yourself and those around you.

When you are ready, you can open your eyes.

Cultivating Joy in 8 Breaths

This guided meditation is a simple yet effective way to increase your overall well-being in just eight short breaths.

Each inhale and exhale is associated with a single word to guide your focus and enhance the experience.

Remember, the 8 breaths in this exercise are merely symbolic and are not a strict requirement. You are free to take as many breaths as you need for each step.

1. Start with the inhale and focus on the physical act of breathing. Repeat the word "**breath**" to yourself and concentrate on the full cycle of inhaling and exhaling, and feel the sensation of air entering and leaving your body.

2. As you take a second breath, pay close attention to every sensation in your body. Be present in the moment and let your awareness permeate every cell. Take note of any good, painful, or neutral sensations you may be experiencing. Try not to modify your feelings and see what happens. This inhale is referred to as "**body**."

3. On the third breath, make a conscious effort to let go of any remaining stress, fatigue, or anxiety. Visualize it leaving your body with each exhaled breath. This sigh of relief is referred to as a "**release**."

4. With the fourth breath, send positive thoughts to yourself. Think kind and loving thoughts toward your brain and body. This is the "**love**" breath.

5. As you take the fifth breath, take stock of any cravings or aversions you may be experiencing. Acknowledge them rather than trying to suppress them. This breath is described as "**desires**."

6. The sixth breath is all about focusing on the present moment. Realize that this moment

contains all the elements necessary for your happiness. There are an endless number of reasons to be happy and an infinite number of reasons to be sad right now. Thinking about where we want to focus can help us make better decisions. This breath is referred to as "**letting go**."

7. On the seventh breath, take a moment to marvel at the gift of life. Recognize the incredible value of the present momentary existence. This breath is referred to as "**alive**."

8. Finally, make the most of your eighth breath by fully appreciating the splendor of your inner and outer worlds. Relax and take it easy as you absorb the beauty of your surroundings. When we stop trying to control our surroundings and start living in the here and now, we realize that reality is breathtaking. Let's just relax and take it easy. This inhale is the epitome of "**beauty**."

Whether you have just a few minutes to spare or a whole hour, take the time to practice these eight breaths to elevate your happiness levels.

Chapter Takeaways

- **Compassionate Body Scan:** This guided meditation helps you to be more kind, accepting, and aware of your physical sensations. By focusing on different parts of your body, you'll learn to observe them without judgment and cultivate a sense of compassion toward yourself.

- **Self-Acceptance:** This meditation is designed to help you learn to accept yourself more fully. Through this practice, you'll come to terms with reality and develop a deeper understanding of your thoughts, emotions, and physical sensations.
- **Healing pain from the past:** This practice aims to release past pain and negative memories that may be holding you back from living in the present. It helps to create space for new experiences and reduce inner and outer conflicts.
- **Cultivate Compassion:** This four-stage process of becoming aware of ourselves, acknowledging that awareness, exploring it, and sitting with it, helps to cultivate a sense of compassion toward ourselves and others.
- **Cultivating joy:** This practice aims to develop a sense of joy and happiness. This guided practice is a quick and easy way to enhance your overall well-being in just a matter of eight breaths.

6. Journey to the Core

You can't change the outside without changing the inside.

— Yong Kang Chan

Trauma is like a shadow that follows us wherever we go, shaping our thoughts, emotions, and actions without us even realizing it. It can be the source of our deepest pain and self-doubt, preventing us from living fulfilling lives. Unresolved traumatic experiences can contribute to negative self-talk, self-doubt, and feelings of worthlessness. These negative thoughts and feelings can make it challenging to be kind and understanding toward ourselves.

This chapter will guide you through the process of uncovering and healing past traumas and beliefs that may be holding you back from living your best life. We will delve into the powerful connection between past trauma and self-compassion and explore how healing past traumas can be the key to unlocking a life of greater happiness, self-acceptance, and inner peace.

Nurturing Your Inner-Child

You may have heard buzzwords like "inner child work," "shadow work," "childhood trauma," and "re-parenting" floating around lately, but don't let the trendiness fool you - these concepts are fundamental when it comes to our personal growth. They are an integral part of our being and play a crucial role in shaping our thoughts, emotions, and actions. Through inner child work, we can learn to heal the emotional wounds and unmet needs of our inner child and help it to grow into a strong, healthy, and well-rounded part of ourselves.

Imagine a young plant that was planted in dry, rocky soil and didn't receive enough water or sunlight. The plant will struggle to grow and likely be stunted and weak. Similarly, if we experience neglect or abuse during childhood, we may struggle to grow emotionally and develop negative behavior patterns or low self-esteem.

Just as a gardener would provide the right amount of water, sunlight, and fertilization, inner child work involves providing your inner child with the proper care by connecting with it in a healthy way and nurturing it through self-compassion. This process involves exploring your past experiences, addressing past traumas, and replacing toxic patterns with positive, nurturing ones.

As adults, we may think that our childhoods were normal and that our parents did the best they could. Childhood trauma can stem from various sources, not just abuse or neglect. Even seemingly innocent family dynamics can leave an imprint on our inner child.

We may not see how the stress and challenges of daily life, like balancing work and family, can affect a child's emotional well-being. But to a child, these situations can be traumatic and leave deep emotional wounds.

These wounds can then be carried into adulthood, affecting our thoughts, emotions, and behaviors, and even passed on to our children. Inner child work allows us to understand and heal these wounds and develop a healthy and loving relationship with ourselves and, subsequently, with others.

Exercise: Connecting with your inner child

- Before we start this meditation, remember that if at any point you feel the need to pause, go ahead and do so. Your experience is unique, and it's important to move at your own pace and be present in each moment. Take all the time you need.
- First, find a comfortable and quiet place where you can relax, focus, and won't be disturbed. Close your eyes and take a deep breath, let go of any distractions and let yourself be fully present in the moment.
- We often believe that our childhood story ends when we become adults, but it doesn't necessarily. Our inner child remains alive within us, carrying the essence of who we once were. No matter how loving or unloving our upbringing was, the child

within us holds a special place in our hearts and in our memories.

- Now go back in time and imagine yourself as a child. Take yourself to a specific age and place that holds special memories. Take a close look at your inner child. How old are they? Notice their physical features, attitude, body language, and overall demeanor. What is your first impression of this child?

- As you focus on this image, pay attention to any emotions or thoughts that come to mind. These may be related to specific memories or experiences from your childhood. Notice your emotions without judging them and return to focusing on your inner child.

- Once you've identified these emotions or thoughts, initiate a conversation with your inner child. Ask them how they're feeling today and what's on their mind. Listen attentively to their response, allowing them to express themselves freely. Show your inner child that they are heard and valued, creating a safe and nurturing space for them to share.

- Now, thank your inner child for their honest answers and offer them comfort and reassurance. Tell your inner child that you understand and are there for them.

- Spend some time in silence, allowing your inner child to express anything else they might want to share. Keep listening attentively and try to understand their perspective. This is your inner child's chance to speak, and it's important to be a good listener.

- When you feel ready, tell your inner child you will work on meeting their needs in healthy ways as an adult. Remember that your inner child is a part of you and needs your love and care. Say goodbye to your inner child and give them a loving embrace.
- Slowly come back from the depths of your internal world and open your eyes.
- Take a moment to journal about your experience. Write down any emotions, thoughts, or insights that came up during the exercise. This will help you reflect on what you've learned and connect with your inner child in the future.

Exercise: Healing Childhood Trauma

Our childhood experiences shape who we are and can affect us profoundly. In this exercise, we'll look within ourselves to face and heal any pain from our past. This journey of self-discovery will help us turn our struggles into strengths and move forward confidently.

Step 1: Setting the Scene

Begin by closing your eyes and taking a few deep breaths. Imagine yourself standing in front of a large door. This door represents the entrance to your healing journey. Take a moment to notice any feelings or sensations that come up for you as you stand in front of this door.

Step 2: Creating Your Guide

Next, imagine that you are creating a guiding companion to help you on your journey. This guide can take any form you like - it could be a person, an animal, or even an object. Consider what qualities you would like your companion to have - for example, are they kind and supportive or strong and protective? Once you have a clear image of your guide in your mind, give them a name and welcome them to your journey.

Step 3: Entering the Healing Forest

With your guide by your side, imagine walking through the door and entering a beautiful forest. This forest represents the different parts of yourself you will be exploring on your journey. Notice the different trees and plants you see – each represents various aspects of your past experiences.

Step 4: Meeting Your Inner Child

As you continue to walk through the forest, you come across a small child sitting on a tree stump. This child represents your inner child - the part of you that experienced the trauma. Notice how the child feels - are they scared, sad, or angry? Take a moment to acknowledge their feelings and let them know you are here to support them.

Step 5: Facing Your Trauma

As you continue to walk through the forest with your guide and inner child, you come across a clearing. In the center of the clearing is a representation of the traumatic event you experienced. It could be a person, a place, or an object. Take a moment to notice how you feel as you approach this representation. Your guide is there to support you and your inner child as you begin to process and work through your trauma.

Step 6: Finding Inner Strength

After some time, you begin to notice that you feel stronger and more empowered. This is because you have faced your trauma and can now move forward. Imagine that you are now leaving the clearing and walking deeper into the forest. As you walk, you come across a tree that represents inner strength. Take a moment to sit underneath this tree and imagine that its strength is flowing into you.

Step 7: Emerging from the Forest

After some time, you come to the edge of the forest. You can see a bright light shining in the distance. This light represents your healing and growth. Take a moment to say goodbye to your guide and inner child, and thank them for their support on your journey. As you step out of the forest, take a moment to notice how you feel - you may feel lighter, more at peace, and more in control of your emotions.

Step 8: Reflecting on your Journey

Take a moment to reflect on your journey and write down any insights or revelations that came up for you during the exercise. Remember that healing is a process and that taking your time is okay. You can revisit this exercise whenever you need to and continue to work through your trauma in a supportive and creative way.

Unveiling the Higher Self

Many of us go through life feeling lost, disconnected, or unfulfilled without realizing that the answers we seek lie within ourselves. Imagine a wise and all-knowing version of yourself who is always by your side, whispering words of wisdom in your ear. Your higher self is always speaking to you, but we are often reluctant to listen to it. Your higher self is the part of you that is in tune with your deepest desires, your highest potential, and your ultimate purpose. It is the voice within that guides you toward your passions and your destiny. It is the compass that points you in the direction of true fulfillment.

Exercise: Unlocking the Secrets of the Soul

- Take a deep breath and close your eyes. Imagine a bright, warm light at the center of your chest. This is the light of your higher self, shining bright and strong.
- Now, focus your attention on the area of your chest. Pay close attention to your senses and keep track of any changes that may indicate that you've made a connection. You might feel a sense of calm, warmth, expansion, or connection. These are all signs that you're on the right track.
- Next, try to locate the source of the feeling. Imagine that your higher self is an actual being you can communicate with. Imagine that you're sitting across from it, looking into its eyes. Imagine that simply being in its presence makes you feel better.
- Now, speak to your higher self. Ask it for guidance, advice, or insight. You might get an idea, a feeling, a symbol, or just a gut feeling as an answer. Don't worry if the solutions you're looking for don't come to you immediately. Sometimes, the answers come in a dream or at a time when you're more emotionally prepared to hear them.

- As you speak to your higher self, pay attention to the way your body feels. Does it feel light and relaxed, or heavy and tense? This can be a sign of whether the advice you're receiving is in alignment with your true self or not.
- When you feel like the conversation is over, thank your higher self for its guidance and open your eyes. Take a moment to reflect on what you've learned, and write it down in your journal. If you feel like the exercise helped, repeat it over the course of several days.
- Remember, connecting with your higher self is not always easy, but it is a journey worth taking. With practice, you'll get better at recognizing the signs of a connection and trusting the guidance you receive. So, keep an open mind, stay patient, and enjoy the adventure!

Receiving validation from within

Validation is essential for our emotional well-being; it helps us feel seen, heard, and understood. But, seeking validation from others can be a futile and never-ending quest, as we are constantly changing and evolving, and what we need to feel validated might also change. That's why it's essential to learn to seek validation from within.

Your higher self is the part of you that is connected to your inner wisdom; it knows what is best for you and what you genuinely need to feel fulfilled. It's the voice inside of you that guides you toward your purpose and helps you navigate through life's challenges. But it's important to note that listening to your higher self takes time and practice.

The following exercise can help you start the process of seeking validation from within.

Exercise

1. Take a few deep breaths and find a quiet place where you can sit comfortably without any distractions.
2. Close your eyes and bring your awareness to your breath. Lay your hands on your heart, on your stomach, or simply by your side.
3. Take a moment to reflect on a time in your life when you sought someone's attention, approval, or acceptance. Pay attention to the initial thoughts that arise and allow yourself to acknowledge them without judgment or dismissiveness.
4. Ask yourself what you would have wished this person would've told you. What kind of validation were you looking for?
5. When you have the answer, ask yourself the following question: Why do I need their approval to feel important, support to feel supported, and love to feel loved?
6. Repeat this question several times, and be open to receiving different answers.
7. Once you have a clear answer, take a moment to reflect on it.
8. Ask yourself: "How can I give myself the validation I need right now?" "What does my body need?" "What can I do to improve my mental and physical health and well-being?"
9. Listen to your inner wisdom and take the necessary steps to give yourself the necessary

validation. If the answers to these questions did not come to you immediately, give it time and keep practicing this meditation.

By regularly practicing this exercise, you will build a deeper connection with your higher self and learn to rely on its guidance for validation.

A letter of Support from Your Higher Self

We all have moments in life when we feel lost, alone, or unsupported, and it can be hard to find the motivation and confidence to keep going when we're in a difficult place. That's why it's crucial to have a source of support that we can always turn to, and that source of support is ourselves.

Our higher self is the part of us that is always there to guide and support us; it knows what is best for us and what we need to hear in difficult times. But sometimes, it can be hard to listen to its guidance, especially when we're feeling down. That's why I want to introduce you to an exercise that can help you get the support you need from your higher self.

Exercise

1. Take a piece of paper and a pen, or open a word document on your computer.
2. Imagine that you have an imaginary friend who is loving, accepting, kind, and caring and who would never judge you or cause you any harm. Think of this person as someone who can see you exactly as you are right now, including the parts of yourself you don't like or keep hidden. Consider how your friend feels about you and how much they love

you despite your flaws. This friend understands that you are human and is gracious and forgiving. This wise companion knows that the sum of your experiences, as countless as they may be, have shaped you into the person you are now.

3. Now, write a letter from this loving person's perspective about how you take care of and talk to yourself. Imagine someone who has boundless compassion, approaches you, and offers advice. How would your friend express their sympathy for you, especially in light of the anguish you experience due to your own severe self-criticism? And if this person were to offer advice about what you should do to improve your life, how do you think they would do so in a way that exemplified unconditional love and kindness?

4. When you're finished, put the letter away and read it the next time you feel down. Take in the words that your friend has to offer. Keep the letter somewhere safe, where you can refer to it whenever you need a reminder of your inner strength and wisdom.

Remember, this exercise can be repeated as often as you need; it's a great tool to help you connect with your higher self and receive the support you need. And remember, you have the inherent right to be loved, connected, and accepted.

Chapter Takeaways

- Trauma can shape our thoughts, emotions, and actions without us realizing it, leading to negative self-talk, self-doubt, and feelings of worthlessness.
- Inner child work is an approach to help heal past traumas and develop a positive relationship with oneself, which in turn improves relationships with others.
- Our higher self is the inner guide that always supports us and knows what's best for us.
- We can learn to nurture and support ourselves without needing external validation by connecting with our inner child and higher self.

7. Compassion in Relationships

You never really understand a person until you consider things from their point of view...until you climb inside of their skin and walk around in it.

— Harper Lee

The journey of self-compassion is a never-ending one, and when we think we have mastered it, we realize there's another layer to uncover. By being more compassionate toward ourselves, we come to realize that we have not been truly able to extend compassion unconditionally to others in the past. It's like we've been walking around with a blindfold on all this time. We couldn't see the good in ourselves, let alone in others. But when we start treating ourselves with kindness and understanding, our blindfold is lifted, and we see the world in a whole new light.

As we become more self-compassionate, we are filling ourselves up with the resources we need to give back to others. We feel better about ourselves and have more energy, patience, and kindness to offer to those around us.

This chapter will explore how self-compassion and being compassionate to others are interconnected. We will discover that compassion and empathy are essential for building stronger relationships and fostering a more peaceful and harmonious world. We will learn how to put ourselves in others' shoes, understand their struggles and joys, and offer them the same kindness and understanding we have learned to offer ourselves.

Compassion In Conflicts

Conflict is an inevitable part of life. Whether with a friend, family member, or coworker, we all have to navigate disagreements and differences of opinion from time to time. But, when conflicts arise, it's easy to get caught up in our own emotions and react in ways that can escalate the situation and cause further harm. And let's face it; we've all been there.

But when we approach conflicts and disagreements with compassion and understanding, we can avoid becoming entrenched in our own positions and instead seek to understand the other person's perspective.

Compassion can be a powerful tool in this process, allowing us to step back, observe the situation without judgment, and approach the conflict with an open mind and a compassionate heart.

Self-compassionate people have a more positive and understanding attitude toward themselves and others regarding mistakes and failures. They understand that everyone is human and imperfect and don't resort to criticizing or blaming themselves or others for errors. Instead, they have a "cushion" of kindness and a selfless motivation to improve themselves. This allows them to take responsibility for their actions and apologize when necessary.

It is natural for people to become defensive and blame others when problems arise as a way to avoid self-criticism and self-loathing. However, self-compassionate people are more self-aware and approach these situations differently by treating themselves and others with the same empathy and kindness. This makes it easier for them to admit their mistakes and work toward finding solutions.

Here are some tips on how to practice compassion for others in conflict situations:

1. **Listen actively:** When you are in a conversation with someone with a different opinion or perspective, try to listen actively to what they have to say. Don't think about how you will respond, and avoid interrupting or dismissing their thoughts. Instead, keep asking questions to gain a deeper understanding of their viewpoint.

2. **Avoid getting defensive:** It's natural to feel defensive when someone challenges our beliefs or opinions. Getting defensive distracts you from feeling hurt or shamed and shifts the focus to the faults of the other. See if you can become aware of defensiveness and create a moment for yourself to nurture any difficult feelings. When you've

acknowledged and validated your feelings try returning to the conversation with an open mind.

3. **Find common ground:** Find areas of agreement and shared values. This can help to build a foundation of understanding and respect.

4. **Stay open to learning and be curious:** Approach the conversation with a mindset of learning and growth rather than trying to convince the other person of your point of view.

5. **Practice empathy:** Try to put yourself in the other person's shoes and understand where they are coming from. Empathy helps to build understanding and connection.

6. **Keep perspective:** Remember that people's opinions and views are often shaped by their experiences and backgrounds, and try not to take things personally.

7. **Respectful disagreement:** It's okay to disagree, and it's important to respect other people's opinions, even if they differ from yours.

The Need for Healthy Boundaries

Healthy relationships are built on a foundation of compassion. However, compassion alone is not enough; it must be balanced with healthy boundaries, or it can lead to co-dependency and neediness.

When we enter into a committed relationship, it can be easy to fall into the trap of thinking that our partner should fulfill all of our emotional needs and alleviate all of our concerns. We may even begin to feel responsible for their happiness and become overly invested in their emotions and well-being. This is co-dependency, a form of compassion gone awry.

Similarly, neediness is another sign that compassion and boundaries are not balanced in a relationship. Needy individuals may fear rejection or abandonment and may become overly dependent on the validation and attention of others. They may struggle to form a sense of self-worth and look to others to validate their worth.

Both co-dependency and neediness can lead to unhealthy dynamics in relationships, where one person becomes overly invested in the emotions and well-being of the other and struggles to set and maintain healthy boundaries to take care of themselves.

It is important to remember that compassion and healthy boundaries are not mutually exclusive. We can have compassion for others while also being aware of our needs and limits. This means learning to practice self-compassion, being kind and understanding toward ourselves, and learning to set and maintain healthy boundaries. It involves saying "no" when necessary, setting limits on the time and energy we spend on others, and taking care of our physical, emotional, and mental well-being.

Compassion is vital to healthy relationships but must be balanced with healthy boundaries. By learning to practice self-compassion and to set and maintain healthy boundaries, we can foster healthier and more fulfilling relationships.

Strategies to Set Healthier Boundaries

Align your boundaries with your values: Consider your personal values and beliefs when setting boundaries. Use them as a guide to help you determine what you are and are not willing to tolerate in your relationships.

Clarify your intentions: Think about what you want to achieve by setting boundaries. This can help guide your decision-making process and ensure that your boundaries align with your goals.

Evaluate existing relationships: Take the time to reflect on your current relationships and identify any areas where you may need to set boundaries. This can help you assess your relationships' health and make necessary changes.

Recognize relationship differences: Different relationships may require different boundaries. For example, you may have stricter boundaries with a close friend than with a co-worker. It's important to understand that boundaries are not one-size-fits-all and should be tailored to each individual relationship.

Practice and patience: Setting and maintaining boundaries can be challenging and may take time and practice. Be patient with yourself and understand that it's a process that requires effort and dedication.

Speak up respectfully: Communication is key when it comes to setting boundaries. Clearly and respectfully express your boundaries to those in your life. Be confident and assertive in your delivery to ensure that your boundaries are understood and respected.

Pay attention to changes: Relationships can change over time, and it's important to consider these changes. Be mindful of any shifts in your relationships and adjust your boundaries as needed to maintain a healthy balance.

Hold your ground: Maintaining healthy boundaries requires consistency and commitment. Be firm in upholding your boundaries, even in difficult situations. Remember, you have the right to set boundaries that protect your mental and emotional well-being.

Compassion in the World

In today's world, we face a growing number of conflicts and divisions between individuals, groups, and societies. From political tensions to social divisions, it can often feel as though the world is becoming more and more polarized.

It has become easy to fall into the trap of judgment and suspicion toward those different from us. We surround ourselves with like-minded individuals, avoid being challenged or exposed to new perspectives, and feel stronger and more certain because of it. However, we must let go of the illusion that certainty is a sign of strength. True strength lies in our ability to be vulnerable, curious, and humble.

By letting go of our need for affirmation, validation, and approval, we can disentangle ourselves from the idea that we always have to be right. Instead, we can focus on understanding others and how to empathize with them. In doing so, we can build trust and cooperation between people, groups, and societies with different opinions and perspectives.

When we are willing to let go of our judgments and assumptions about others and practice compassion, we open ourselves up to a world of possibilities. We let go of judgment and invite curiosity; we learn to see things from different angles and challenge our beliefs, leading us to a deeper understanding and connection with those around us.

While judgment closes us off to new ideas and perspectives, curiosity opens us up to discovery and exploration. It allows us to see the nuances and complexities in a situation and challenges us to question our assumptions. It's in this state of curiosity that real growth and understanding can occur.

So how do we put this into practice? By following the core principles of self-compassion and applying them to others.

Self-awareness: Self-compassion helps increase self-awareness, allowing you to recognize and understand your thoughts and emotions without judging them. We have become better at identifying and labeling our emotions, understanding how they affect our thoughts and behaviors, and recognizing the triggers that lead to negativity. This can help you approach conversations more clearly, better understand the complexity of the other person's thoughts and emotions, and prevent you from getting defensive.

Emotional regulation: Self-compassion helps to regulate emotions, which can be beneficial when encountering people with different opinions or perspectives. It allows you to have a calm and rational conversation with them rather than getting into a fight or argument. It also helps you to understand where they are coming from and to find common ground.

Perspective-taking: Self-compassion fosters an attitude of perspective-taking, which can be helpful when interacting with people with different opinions or perspectives.

It allows you to understand where the other person is coming from and empathize with their viewpoint, even if you disagree with it. It also helps you to communicate your perspective more effectively, as you can anticipate and address any potential points of contention.

Avoiding perfectionism: Self-compassion helps to avoid perfectionism, the need to be right all the time and always be understood. You become more open to new ideas, and less likely to get stuck in your own point of view. This mindset can help with feeling less attacked and increase the willingness to learn from the other person.

Self-forgiveness: Self-forgiveness allows you to let go of any guilt or negative feelings you may have toward yourself for not understanding or agreeing with others. By forgiving yourself, you can approach the situation with a more open and curious mindset rather than feeling offended or angry. This can lead to more productive and understanding conversations and help reduce any stress or tension you may feel. By being more self-forgiving, you will also be more understanding of the other person and their mistakes and limitations.

Chapter Takeaways

- Practicing self-compassion gives us more energy, patience, and kindness to offer to others, resulting in more positive relationships.
- Approaching conflicts with compassion and understanding leads to a more positive and productive outcome.

- Self-compassion and healthy boundaries are crucial to fostering positive and fulfilling relationships.
- We can build trust, cooperation, and understanding with people and groups that have different opinions and perspectives by using the core principles of self-compassion.

8. Self-Compassionate Parenting

I have found that self-compassion is essential to being fully alive and present, as well as the best antidote to despair.

— Karen Armstrong

Raising little humans can be one wild ride. It's a mix of heartwarming moments and head-scratching moments. You'll find yourself being patient one moment and being tested the next. You'll feel like you're on top of the world when you see your child achieving something new and feel like the worst parent in the world when you can't get them to do something. As much as we love our children, the reality is that parenting can be incredibly challenging. We feel exhausted, anxious, and worried and may feel like we are not doing a good job or living up to our expectations. Fortunately, the practice of self-compassion can help us navigate these challenges and find a way to parent with joy, happiness, and exuberance.

Self-compassionate parenting is about shifting our focus from constantly trying to fix or change ourselves and nurture ourselves so we can be the best parents possible. It is about recognizing that we are all doing our best and need to care for our well-being to support our children better.

This chapter will explore the concept of self-compassionate parenting and how it can help us to be happier, more patient, and more understanding parents. We will discuss the importance of self-care, self-compassion, and self-kindness in parenting and provide practical tips and strategies for incorporating these practices into our daily lives. We will also explore the benefits of self-compassionate parenting for both parents and children, including improved physical and mental health, reduced stress, and better parent-child relationships.

The Challenges of Parenting

One of the most significant challenges of parenting is the constant self-evaluation and criticism that parents place on themselves. This self-judgment can manifest in feelings of inadequacy, low self-esteem, and frustration toward both ourselves and our children.

Some of us might criticize ourselves for not being the perfect parent, making mistakes, or not having all the answers. We feel the need to have the perfect home, the perfect family, and the perfect children. But deep down, we all know that perfection is unattainable, and the constant pursuit of it can lead to feelings of disappointment and failure.

It's important to remember that parenting challenges are typical and expected and that every parent goes through difficult times. Building a sense of community with other parents who understand the trials and tribulations of parenting can provide powerful support and alleviate feelings of isolation, guilt, and blame. We can receive genuine support and understanding by opening up about our struggles and finding someone who can truly empathize with us.

Parents must understand that their own struggles are often reflected in their children's struggles. By prioritizing self-care, they can better provide the support and guidance their child needs.

The Importance of Self-compassionate Parenting

Studies have shown that parents who practice self-care and self-compassion have better physical and mental health, are more confident in their parenting, and have more positive interactions with their children. Self-compassion is associated with lower levels of parental depression and parenting stress, as well as reduced fatigue. By treating themselves with kindness, understanding, and forgiveness, parents set an important example for their children, showing them how to be compassionate and resilient in the face of life's challenges.

One of the key benefits of self-compassionate parenting is that it can help children develop a strong sense of self-worth. When children see their parents treating themselves with kindness and understanding, they learn that they too are worthy of love and respect. This can help them build a positive self-image, which is essential for their emotional and mental well-being.

Another great benefit of self-compassionate parenting is the development of resilience. Children who see their parents handling difficult situations with compassion and understanding are more likely to learn how to cope with their own challenges in a healthy and effective way. They learn that it's okay to make mistakes and that they can bounce back from setbacks.

Self-compassionate parenting can also help children build solid and meaningful connections with others, which is essential for their social and emotional development. When children see their parents treating themselves and others with kindness and understanding, they learn the importance of empathy and compassion in their own relationships.

Practicing Self-Compassion in Parenting

Teaching children the concepts of self-compassion can help them navigate the challenges of life with more joy and happiness. Parents can play an essential role in helping their children develop self-compassion by setting an example and providing guidance.

Here are some tips for introducing the concepts of self-compassion into parenting and helping children develop a self-compassionate mindset.

- Have your child think about a time when they were hard on themselves or felt guilty about something. Ask them how they would feel if a friend came to them with the same problem. Encourage your child to talk about how they would respond and what advice they would give to their friend.

- Explain to your child that it's normal to experience strong emotions such as sadness, frustration, or disappointment. Provide reassurance that these feelings are valid and acceptable and avoid dismissing how they're feeling in that moment. Offer encouragement, such as saying "I understand that you're upset. It's okay to feel that way. Sometimes things don't go as we plan."

- Teach your child the value of forgiveness, both for themselves and others. Show that mistakes are a natural part of life and that letting go and moving forward is important. Express empathy, for example, by saying, "I know you didn't mean to break that. Accidents happen, and it's okay."

- Have your child practice talking to themselves in a supportive and friendly tone, using the advice they would give to a friend. Encourage them to repeat a positive affirmation or mantra that they come up with, such as "I am doing my best" or "I am worthy of love and kindness."

- Acknowledge and praise your child when they show compassion towards themselves. Emphasize how important it is to be kind and understanding. Offer words of encouragement like "I'm proud of you for being so understanding and giving yourself another chance." This helps build their self-compassion and reinforces the idea of treating oneself with love and kindness.

- Practice self-care together. Encourage your child to take time for activities they enjoy, such as reading, sports, or music.
- Help your child to develop a daily self-compassion practice. Encourage them to spend some time each day focusing on the positive aspects of their life and themselves. You can even make a habit of listing some of the things you appreciate about your child before bedtime and letting them do the same thing.

Remember that self-compassion is an ongoing practice that requires consistency and patience. But with your guidance, your child will learn to be kinder and more understanding of themselves and be better equipped to handle life's challenges with more joy and happiness.

Chapter Takeaways

- Self-compassionate parenting is about nurturing ourselves, recognizing that we are all doing our best, and prioritizing our own well-being in order to better support and guide our children.
- Self-care and self-love are essential for effective parenting as it helps parents to understand and address their struggles.
- Self-compassionate parenting has many benefits for both parents and children, such as better mental and physical health, more positive

interactions, and the development of self-worth, resilience, and connections with others.

- With proper guidance, children can learn to be more compassionate toward themselves, making them more resilient and better able to handle life's challenges with happiness and joy.

9. The Nurturing Power of Self-Care

Our sorrows and wounds are only healed when we touch them with compassion.

— Buddha

When you're feeling like you're about to go off a cliff and into the depths of despair, self-care can be an excellent intervention tool that quickly pulls you back up. Contrary to popular belief, self-care is more than just bubble baths and face masks; it's about taking care of yourself on a deeper level. It's about nourishing your mind, body, and soul. It brings you joy and peace just because you're making time for yourself and engaging in activities that make you happy.

A Guide to the Practice of Self-Care

Self-care is essential for our overall happiness and mental health. It is the process of taking an active role in protecting our well-being and is an essential aspect of self-regulation and self-compassion. In the past, it was believed that our brains were hardwired and unchangeable, but recent studies have shown that the brain is malleable and can be rewired.

One way to move past our primitive 'fight-or-flight'-response is by prioritizing self-care and making a conscious decision to adopt two alternative responses: empathy and action. Empathy is the ability to understand and share the feelings of others, and action is taking steps to address the problem and improve the situation.

Experts recommend the following three ways to take care of yourself:

1. Refuel, refresh, and get ready to act. Taking a break from the constant stimulation of the news, social media, and other distractions is important. By switching off the TV, logging out of social media, and disabling alerts and push notifications, you can improve your concentration and spend some time in peace and quiet.
2. Learn to identify the signs that indicate you need to take care of yourself and act accordingly. Taking care of yourself can positively affect your relationships with others. For example, when you need to ask a coworker to cover for you or a babysitter to watch the children. It is important to listen to your body and mind, and recognize when you need rest, relaxation, or self-care. Remember that in the end, taking care of yourself not only benefits you but also improves your relationships with others.

3. Create a self-care checklist with a wide variety of items that you can choose from. A bubble bath or a midday phone call with a friend are just two examples of the many self-care activities you can choose from. If you're on the verge of burnout, you should have this list prepared in case you suddenly find yourself unable to think of any solutions. We will further dive into this later in this chapter.

Admitting you need help is a courageous act of self-care. Remember, self-care is an ongoing process, and it's important to take your time. By prioritizing self-care, you can rewire your brain to adopt more positive and effective responses to stress and adversity.

The Need for a Self-Care Strategy

A self-care plan is a personalized blueprint for taking care of yourself physically and emotionally. It's a roadmap that guides you through difficult times, providing you with the tools and resources to navigate life's challenges.

Creating a personalized self-care plan is a preventative measure that can help you proactively address the stresses of life. By taking the time to consider your needs and the resources you have at your disposal, you can create a plan that will guide you through difficult times with ease. Only you know the limits of your stress and the extent to which you have support at your disposal, so a self-care plan tailored to your unique needs is essential.

Having a plan in place for self-care removes the need for impromptu decision-making when facing adversity. From the perspective of awareness, this allows you to act instead of react. Having a strategy in place might help you feel less stressed and more in command of your life. Telling others about your plans before you seek help makes the process much simpler. This can be helpful in case of emergency or worst-case scenario.

A self-care plan can also help you stay on track. It will be much less of a struggle for you to stick to your self-care plan and avoid giving in to the excuse-making trap. If you and your self-care friend are serious about preventing isolation, planning regular get-togethers can help. You can share the duty of helping one another and checking in with one another regularly. This can be a great way to remind yourself that you're not alone in your struggles and that there are people who care about you and want to help.

Creating a self-care plan can also help you avoid falling into negative patterns and equip you with the necessary skills to handle stressful situations and challenging life events. It provides you with a set of coping mechanisms that can help you manage and navigate these difficult times, keeping you grounded and in control.

Creating Your Self-Care Plan

Self-care is essential for our overall well-being, but creating a personalized self-care plan can be overwhelming. Follow these five steps to create a self-care plan tailored to your individual needs and start taking care of yourself proactively and intentionally.

Step 1: Take a look at your current habits

Before making your self-care plan, taking a good look at where you are now is essential. Reflect on the strategies you currently use to deal with life's demands. Do you go for a walk to relieve stress or tend to withdraw from your friends and family? Do you have a glass of wine after a tough day at work or take a long bath to relieve tension? Write down an honest inventory of your positive and negative coping strategies. This step will help you identify any harmful habits and your existing self-care practices.

Step 2: Identify your self-care needs

Now that you better understand your current habits, it's time to think about what you value most in your day-to-day life. Make a list of all your physical, mental, emotional, and professional needs. A good self-care plan should consider all areas of well-being. This step may be a real eye-opener, you may discover you're already meeting your physical needs, but you're neglecting your emotional needs.

Here are some examples of different types of needs to help you along:

Physical Needs

- Eating a balanced diet
- Getting enough sleep
- Regular exercise
- Managing chronic health conditions
- Preventive health care, such as regular check-ups and screenings
- Taking medications as prescribed

Mental Needs

- Managing stress
- Finding time for hobbies and leisure activities

- Practicing mindfulness or meditation
- Engaging in creative activities
- Learning new skills
- Accessing mental health care as needed

Emotional Needs

- Building and maintaining positive relationships
- Finding a sense of belonging and connection
- Expressing emotions in a healthy way
- Finding healthy ways to cope with difficult emotions
- Setting boundaries and assertively communicating needs

Professional Needs

- Building a career or pursuing further education
- Setting and achieving personal and professional goals
- Networking and building relationships in the industry
- Continuously learning and developing new skills
- Finding work-life balance
- Finding job satisfaction and fulfillment

Step 3: Write down practices that support your needs

It's time to decide which self-care activities will help you meet your needs. Consider asking yourself questions like 'What activities bring me joy?' 'What helps me feel energized?' 'What makes me feel fulfilled?' 'What's helped me cope with difficult moments in my life?' Write down the self-care practices you plan to do daily and those you'll only do once in a while. For example, you'll want to eat healthy daily, but you may only schedule dinner with a friend once a week.

Step 4: Fit your activities into your schedule

Now it's time to find pockets of time throughout your busy day to incorporate these practices. Remember, self-care isn't selfish; it's an act of kindness to yourself. Instead of jamming all sorts of activities into your day, start small. Add one to two activities into your routine each week, and before you know it, you'll have a full-fledged self-care routine. Prioritize the practices you need and value the most, and evaluate how they're helping you improve yourself.

Step 5: Remove any barriers

It's time to let go of any negative habits that are getting in the way of your self-care plan. Replace them with self-care practices, and don't be afraid to ask for help from your friends or family members. Sharing your self-care plan with a supportive network can help you overcome obstacles more easily. And remember, self-care is an ongoing process, so update and adapt your plan as needed.

Claiming Your Healing Time

Incorporating self-care into our daily routine is crucial for maintaining our physical, mental, emotional, and spiritual wellness. It's easy to get caught up in the hustle and bustle of daily life and neglect our own needs. But just like a car needs fuel to function, we, too, need to take care of ourselves to keep going.

Think of the low fuel warning light on your car's dashboard. When it comes on, you know you have a limited amount of time before you'll have to stop and refuel. The same is true for our well-being. We must pay attention to the warning signs that we're running low on energy and take steps to refill our tanks before it's too late.

Try being completely honest with a trusted friend or loved one about your needs, whether it's a need for space or support. Sharing your thoughts and feelings with someone you trust can alleviate some of the stress preventing you from taking care of yourself. Trust me, when you open up and share your thoughts and feelings with someone you trust, you will find an understanding and supportive listener who will be there for you.

Let's revisit the "low fuel" signal on your car's dashboard. When your warning light turns on, it's important not to ignore it. There's also no need to panic or waste energy worrying since you probably still have about 30 miles worth of gas left. If you feel like you're reaching a point of exhaustion or burnout, it's important to immediately take action and reach out to people you trust before reaching a boiling point. Address minor issues before they become bigger problems.

Don't be afraid to reach out and ask for what you need. It's in our nature to be helpful and kind to one another. We're wired to have empathy and feel good when we do good things for others. That's why acts of kindness happen all around us every day. So, it's safe to assume that plenty of people in your life would have been more than happy to lend a helping hand if only they were asked. The problem isn't their willingness to help; it's our hesitance to ask.

Self-Compassion at Work

Let's face it; when it comes to our job performance, we can be our own harshest critics. It's like a switch flips as soon as we step into the office - all the self-compassion and forgiveness we practice in our personal lives go out the window. We put ourselves under a microscope and expect nothing short of perfection - handling all the pressure and stress like a pro, never missing a beat, and always on our A-game. But even at work, we must remind ourselves to be kind and recognize that we all make mistakes and have weaknesses.

In this book, we have delved deeply into strategies for cultivating self-compassion, equipping you with the tools to apply them in the workplace. To remind you of some strategies to help achieve this, here are four ways to cultivate self-compassion at work.

1. **Prioritize self-care:** It's easy to neglect our needs when busy, but taking care of ourselves is essential for our well-being. Make time for activities that nourish your body, mind, and spirit, such as eating well, going for a walk, and connecting with colleagues. And don't be afraid to take a break when you need one.

2. **Embrace your imperfections:** We all have moments of self-doubt and feelings of imposter syndrome, but it's important to remember that everyone experiences these things. Recognize that you are not alone in your struggles and that your imperfections do not define you.

3. **Be kind to yourself:** It only makes things worse when we're hard on ourselves. Instead,

consider yourself a friend in need and offer yourself the same encouragement and support you would give to someone else.

4. **Ask for help:** We often feel that we should be able to handle everything on our own, but that is just not realistic. Remember that it's okay to ask for help and that others will often be happy to support you.

Chapter Takeaways

- Self-care is not just about pampering yourself; it's about taking action to improve your overall well-being on a physical, mental, emotional, and professional level.
- A self-care plan is necessary to address and manage stress and adversity proactively.
- Self-care strategies equip us with healthier coping skills and avoid falling into harmful habits.
- We must stop being extra hard on ourselves at work and acknowledge that we can make mistakes and will always have weaknesses.

10. Transforming Your Mindset with Affirmations

Most unhappy people need to learn just one lesson: how to see themselves through the lens of genuine compassion and treat themselves accordingly.

— Martha Beck

Thoughts are powerful things, shaping our perception of the world and influencing our actions and decisions. Our thoughts are like a lens through which we view the world, and they can either limit or expand our possibilities.

How we think about ourselves, our abilities, and our circumstances can profoundly affect our reality. For example, if we believe we can succeed in a particular endeavor, we are more likely to take the necessary steps to achieve that success. On the other hand, if we believe we are not capable or that success is not possible, we are less likely to take action.

Our thoughts also shape our emotional state. Positive thoughts can lead to happiness, motivation, and contentment, while negative thinking leads to sadness, hopelessness, and frustration. Our emotions, in turn, influence our behavior and actions.

It is important to note that thoughts aren't simply random musings; they are closely connected to our beliefs and experiences, and our past shapes them. We can learn to change negative thoughts and ideas to create a new reality that aligns with our goals and values.

Affirmations are a powerful tool to help us align our thoughts and comments with our intentions and manifest the life we desire. They help purify our thoughts, restructure our mindsets, and can help make us believe anything is possible. With regular use, affirmations can help us to achieve our goals, build self-confidence and ultimately, live our best lives.

How Do Affirmations Work?

Our thoughts are connected to specific paths in our heads. Just like electricity travels through circuits, our thoughts travel through these paths in our brains. When we think the same thing over and over, it gets easier for our brain to think that way, and it becomes a habit. This happens even if the thought is not a good or correct one. Instead of allowing our heads to overflow with negative thoughts, we can actively choose to counter those thoughts with positive affirmations.

Great thinkers, successful businesspeople, and spiritual leaders have used affirmations for centuries. They are a simple yet powerful tool that can help us overcome limiting beliefs, build self-confidence, and even manifest our wildest dreams. But affirmations aren't just for the elite few, they're for anyone who wants to improve their lives and achieve their goals.

Affirmations work by reprogramming our subconscious mind. Our subconscious mind is the part of our brain that controls our automatic thoughts and actions. It is responsible for many of our habits and beliefs and is often the source of negative thoughts and self-doubt. By repeating affirmations, we are giving our subconscious mind new information to process and new views to adopt. This can help to replace negative thoughts and ideas with positive ones.

Making sure the affirmations you're using resonate with you, is very important, as this will help you connect to them emotionally. To build belief, try visualizing the affirmation as if it's already happened, and imagine yourself living it. When negative thoughts come up, counteract them with positive affirmations. Over time, this can help change negative patterns of thinking.

Affirmations are most effective when they are specific, personal, and written in the present tense. For example, instead of saying, "I will be successful," it's more effective to say, "I am successful." This helps to create a sense of immediacy and makes the affirmation feel more natural.

If you're initially skeptical about positive affirmations, don't worry - you're not alone. Many people are hesitant to try affirmations, but in many cases, that has to do with a misunderstanding of their purpose. It's important to understand that positive affirmations are not a standalone solution for achieving our desires. Simply repeating affirmations alone will not bring about change.

To fully benefit from affirmations, they must be accompanied by intentional action and effort. Affirmations serve as a catalyst for setting our intentions, but it's up to us to put in the work to make those aspirations a reality. Consider affirmations as the starting engine - they provide the initial push, but it's up to us to keep moving towards our destination.

How to Practice Affirmations

- **Choose your affirmations:** Select affirmations that resonate with you and align with your goals and values. Make sure they are specific, personal, and written in the present tense. You will find a list of self-compassion affirmations below that you can personalize and make your own.
- **Write them down:** Write your affirmations on paper or in a journal. Having them written down can help make them feel more natural and increase their effectiveness.
- **Repeat them regularly:** Repeat your affirmations to yourself multiple times a day. It's best to repeat them when you first wake up and before bed, but you can also repeat them throughout the day as needed. It may take some time to notice a change, so be patient and keep at it.
- **Say them with conviction:** When you repeat your affirmations, say them with conviction and

believe in them. Speak them out loud or in your mind with enthusiasm and emotion.

- **Visualize:** Visualize yourself already having achieved the things you want to achieve while you are saying the affirmations.
- **Track your progress:** Keep track of your progress by noting any changes you notice in your thoughts, feelings, or behaviors. This will help you see the impact of your affirmations and keep you motivated to continue.

Self-Compassion Affirmations

1. I am kind and compassionate toward myself.
2. I treat myself with the same care and understanding I would offer to a good friend.
3. I am worthy of love and acceptance, including my own.
4. I am allowed to make mistakes and learn from them.
5. I am patient and understanding with myself.
6. I accept my imperfections and celebrate my strengths.
7. I am worthy of self-care and self-nurturing.
8. I am strong and capable of handling difficult emotions.
9. I trust my inner wisdom and intuition.
10. I give myself permission to feel and process my emotions.
11. I am enough, just as I am.
12. I let go of self-criticism and embrace self-compassion.

13. I am open to learning and growing from my experiences.
14. I am not defined by my past mistakes or failures.
15. I am deserving of a fulfilling and happy life.
16. I am kind to myself in my thoughts and actions.
17. I am grateful for my unique qualities and talents.
18. I am willing to forgive myself for past mistakes.
19. I trust in my ability to heal and grow.
20. I am worthy of respect and dignity, including my own.
21. I choose to focus on my positive qualities and strengths.
22. I am compassionate toward myself in times of stress and struggle.
23. I am patient with my progress and trust the journey of self-improvement.
24. I am not alone in my struggles, and seek support when needed.
25. I am proud of my accomplishments and recognize my efforts.
26. I am open to learning from my mistakes and taking responsibility for my actions.
27. I am kind to myself and practice self-care regularly.
28. I recognize my worth and value as a human being.
29. I choose to be gentle and understanding with myself.
30. I am willing to let go of self-doubt and trust in my abilities.
31. I am capable of change and growth.
32. I am compassionate toward myself and others.
33. I am grateful for the opportunity to learn and improve.

34. I am worthy of a fulfilling and satisfying life.
35. I practice self-compassion daily and strive to be my best self.

Conclusion

The journey of self-compassion is a powerful and transformative one. By learning to be kind, gentle, and understanding with ourselves, we unlock the full potential of our minds and hearts. Through the practice of self-compassion, we learn to embrace our humanity, accept our flaws and imperfections, and live life to the fullest.

We come to understand that our self-worth is not dependent on our achievements or failures, but rather on our inherent value as human beings. We all have value, and we all deserve kindness, no matter what. Self-compassion allows us to release the grip of negative self-criticism and replace it with a sense of calm and interconnected acceptance, turning anguish into happiness.

This book has explored the various aspects of self-compassion and how it can be applied in our daily lives. We began by explaining the concept of self-compassion and recognizing self-criticism. We delved into practical exercises and meditations to help us cultivate self-compassion in our daily lives. We explored how self-compassion can help us be more resilient, cope with stress and anxiety, improve our relationships, and find meaning and purpose in our lives. We also saw how it can help us overcome perfectionism and be more creative. By learning to be more compassionate with ourselves, we have developed more compassion for others and, in the end, are able to create a more compassionate world.

Learning self-compassion is like learning a new language. Just like you wouldn't become fluent in a new language by simply acknowledging its existence, you won't develop self-compassion without consistent practice. To develop self-compassion, it's important to keep paying attention to the things you tell yourself, especially when times are rough.

Self-compassion is a life-changing expedition that requires determination and hard work, but the rewards are beyond measure. This book serves as your compass, providing the tools and guidance needed to embark on a journey of self-discovery and growth. By practicing self-awareness, self-care, and compassion, you will not only transform your relationship with yourself, but also the way you interact with the world around you. Embrace the journey with open arms and a curious spirit and I'm sure you will be pleasantly surprised at where it might take you.

Thank You

Thank you so much for buying my book. I hope it was both informative and insightful.

Before you go, can I ask you for one small favor? **Could you please consider leaving a review on Amazon?**

Your feedback helps independent authors like me to create more books that will hopefully keep on helping you and others.

It would mean the world to me to hear from you.

Get Your Ebook Stop Limiting Yourself
+ Reduce Stress in 1 minute [video]
+ Printable Gratitude Journal

 +  +

Scan the QR code below to claim your free bonuses

—————————— **OR** ——————————

visit gifts.zerayoung.com/compassion

Unleash your true potential and choose to live your best life!

✔Free e-book: Stop Limiting Yourself. Stop doubting your potential and learn to recognize your self-limiting beliefs!

✔Free meditation video: Reduce your stress levels in one minute with this powerful breathing exercise.

✔Printable Journal: Print out your daily and monthly Personal Gratitude Journal for positive manifestation and improved self-confidence!

References

Abblett, M. (2022, January 10). *Mindful Parenting: Meet Your Inner Critic with Self-Compassion.* Mindful. https://www.mindful.org/mindful-parenting-meet-your-inner-critic-with-self-compassion/

Baulch, J. (2022, February 8). *Why is Self-Compassion so Hard Sometimes?* Inner Melbourne Psychology. https://www.innermelbpsychology.com.au/why-is-self-compassion-so-hard-sometimes/

Breines, J. G., & Chen, S. (2012). *Self-compassion increases self-improvement motivation.* Personality and Social Psychology Bulletin, 38(9), 1133-1143.

Breines, J. G., & Chen, S. (2013). *Self-compassion and well-being in China: An examination of the mediating role of mindfulness.* Self and Identity, 12(1), 78-98.

Center for Mindful Self-Compassion. (2020, November 18). *What is Self-Compassion?* CMSC. https://centerformsc.org/learn-msc/

Chowdhury, R. B. M. A. (2022, September 12). *What Is Loving-Kindness Meditation?* (Incl. Scripts). PositivePsychology.com. https://positivepsychology.com/loving-kindness-meditation/

Coelho, S. (2022, September 7). *The Benefits of Self-Compassion.* Psych Central. https://psychcentral.com/blog/practicing-self-compassion-when-you-have-a-mental-illness

Colasacco, E. (2022, January 11). *Befriend Your Body: A Compassionate Body Scan. The on Being Project.* https://onbeing.org/blog/befriend-your-body-a-compassionate-body-scan/

Cratsley, R. F. (2023, January 3). *A Guided Meditation for Healing Through Hope.* Mindful. https://www.mindful.org/a-12-minute-meditation-for-healing-through-hope/

Davenport, B. (2022, August 26). *Follow This Self-Love Meditation Script To Treat Yourself With Compassion.* Mindful Zen. https://mindfulzen.co/self-love-meditation/

Davis, W. (2020, October 21). *Self-Compassionate Parenting.* Postpartum Support International (PSI). https://www.postpartum.net/self-compassionate-parenting/

Definition and Three Elements of Self Compassion | Kristin Neff. (2020, July 9). Self-Compassion. https://self-compassion.org/the-three-elements-of-self-compassion-2/

Germer, C. K. (2009). *The mindful path to self-compassion: Freeing yourself from destructive thoughts and emotions.* Guilford Press.

Gilbert, P., & Proctor, S. (2006). *Compassionate mind training for people with high shame and self-criticism: Overview and pilot study of a group therapy approach.* Clinical Psychology & Psychotherapy, 13(6), 353-379.

GoodTherapy Editor Team. (n.d.). *Self-Compassion.* https://www.goodtherapy.org/learn-about-therapy/issues/self-compassion

Hardy, J. (2021, June 17). *How to Practice Loving-Kindness.* Lions Roar. https://www.lionsroar.com/how-to-practice-loving-kindness/

Hendershot, C. (2022, March 18). *Meeting Difficult Emotions with Compassion.* Grand Rapids Center for Mindfulness. https://www.grandrapidscenterformindfulness.com/meet-difficult-emotions-with-compassion/

How to Practice Loving Kindness Meditation. (2020, February 11). Verywell Mind. https://www.verywellmind.com/how-to-practice-loving-kindness-meditation-3144786

Jones, C. (2023, January 10). *A 15-Minute Meditation for Self-Acceptance.* Mindful. https://www.mindful.org/a-15-minute-meditation-for-self-acceptance/

Just a moment. (n.d.). https://yogainternational.com/article/view/guided-meditation-for-self-love/

Kabat-Zinn, J. (2022, October 4). *This Loving-Kindness Meditation is a Radical Act of Love.* Mindful. https://www.mindful.org/this-loving-kindness-meditation-is-a-radical-act-of-love/

Kramer, J. (2021, November 8). *The benefits of self-compassion and how to cultivate it for yourself.* Centres for Health and Healing. https://cfhh.ca/blog/the-benefits-of-self-compassion/

Kuyken, W. (2022, January 18). *Sparking Joy: A Mindfulness Practice for Everyday.* Mindful. https://www.mindful.org/sparking-joy-a-mindfulness-practice-for-everyday/

Leary, M. R., Tate, E. B., Adams, C. E., Batts Allen, A., & Hancock, J. (2007). *Self-compassion and reactions to unpleasant self-relevant events: The implications of treating oneself kindly.* Journal of Personality and Social Psychology, 92(5), 887-904.

MacBeth, A., & Gumley, A. (2012). *Exploring compassion: A meta-analysis of the association between self-compassion and psychopathology.* Clinical Psychology Review, 32(6), 545-552.

Maldonado, M. (2021, November 16). *A Guided RAIN Meditation to Cultivate Compassion.* Mindful. https://www.mindful.org/a-guided-rain-meditation-to-cultivate-compassion/

Mangotich, H. S. T. (2020, October 15). *When Self Compassion is Hard.*

Psychotherapytoronto.   https://www.psychotherapyinthecity.-com/post/when-self-compassion-is-hard

Medcalf, A. (2020, February 18). *IS SELF-COMPASSION THE SECRET TO A HAPPY RELATIONSHIP?* Abby Medcalf. https://abbymedcalf.-com/is-self-compassion-the-secret-to-a-happy-relationship/

Megginson, M. (2022, February 3). *Why Self-Compassion Is Key to a Better Relationship.* The Center. https://www.thecenterportland.com/why-self-compassion-is-key-to-a-better-relationship/

Mental Health and Self-Care. (n.d.). Priory. https://www.priorygroup.-com/blog/mental-health-and-self-care

Neff, K. D. (2003). *The development and validation of a scale to measure self-compassion.* Self and Identity, 2(3), 223-250.

Neff, K. D., & Germer, C. K. (2013). *A pilot study and randomized controlled trial of the mindful self-compassion program.* Journal of Clinical Psychology, 69(1), 28-44.

O'Brien, E. (2022, March 10). *Why Is It So Hard to Practice Self-Compassion?* Yoga Journal. https://www.yogajournal.com/lifestyle/why-is-it-hard-to-practice-self-compassion/

O'Leary, W. (2021, December 13). *7 Self-Compassion Reminders for Parents of Kids Who Are Struggling.* Mindful. https://www.mindful.org/7-self-compassion-reminders-for-parents-of-kids-who-are-struggling/

Parker, T. (n.d.). *Self-Compassion In Relationships.* http://thrivingrelation-ships.org/cultivate-compassion/self-compassion-in-relationships/

Redd, K. (2021, February 18). *7 Concrete Ways Self-Compassion Can Improve Your Marriage.* Marriage Advice - Expert Marriage Tips & Advice.   https://www.marriage.com/advice/relationship/self-compas-sion-can-improve-your-marriage/

Ribeiro, M. B. (2022, August 13). *What Is Compassion Meditation? (+ Mantras and Scripts).* PositivePsychology.com. https://positivepsycholo-gy.com/compassion-meditation/

Salzberg, S. (2022, January 19). *Why Loving-Kindness Takes Time: Sharon Salzberg.*   Mindful.   https://www.mindful.org/loving-kindness-takes-time-sharon-salzberg/

Staff, M. (2022, July 6). *A Guide to Practicing Self-Care with Mindfulness.* Mindful. https://www.mindful.org/a-guide-to-practicing-self-care-with-mindfulness/

Suraliya, S. (2022, December 2). *5 Life-Changing Benefits of Self-Compas-sion.* Your Mental Health Pal. https://yourmentalhealthpal.com/bene-fits-of-self-compassion/

The hidden benefits of self-compassion. (n.d.). https://www.betterup.-com/blog/hidden-benefits-of-self-compassion

Tusa, S. (2020, July 28). *Joy Is a Radical Act. Tricycle: The Buddhist Review.*
    https://tricycle.org/article/joy-meditation/

What   is   Self-Compassion?   (2016,   January   1).   GoStrengths!
    https://gostrengths.com/what-is-self-compassion/

Why Is Self-Compassion So Hard for Some People? (n.d.). Greater Good.
    https://greatergood.berkeley.edu/article/item/why_is_self_compassion_-
    so_hard_for_some_people